ENGLISH Heritage has petitioned the House of Lords to amend the Channel Tunnel Rail Link Bill to include protection for the listed buildings at King's Cross, including the Victorian gasometers above, and Sir George Gilbert Scott's magnificent Gothic railway hotel, *writes Maev Kennedy*.

English Heritage has acted after months of private negotiations with the rail link developers, London and Continental Railways, failed to guarantee the future of the buildings.

Tomorrow is the closing date for petitions to the Lords on the bill.

St Pancras Chambers, the former Midland Grand Hotel, which has recently been partly restored using over £10 million in public money, is Grade I listed and would normally have the highest protection against unsympathetic alteration. However, the Channel Tunnel bill specifically dispenses with the usual planning and listed building controls.

The three Grade II listed Victorian gas-holders are much more vulnera-

rail terminal. English Heritage proposes they should be dismantled, and rebuilt, along with the locomotive watering point which dates from the steam age.

The proposals would require London and Continental Railways to find an appropriate use for the St Pancras Chambers within two years of the terminal opening, or to offer it for sale.

PHOTOGRAPH: GRAHAM TURNER

Change at
KING'S CROSS

Editors:
Michael Hunter
Robert Thorne

Contributors:
Gordon Biddle
Oliver Carter
Stephen Duckworth
Alan Faulkner

Michael Hunter
Barry Jones
Gavin Stamp
Robert Thorne

HISTORICAL PUBLICATIONS

Change at KING'S CROSS
From 1800 to the Present

THE ILLUSTRATIONS

The following have kindly given their permission to reproduce illustrations:

Builder Index Project, *15, 33, 35*
Camden Local History Library, *9, 58, 59, 62, 72*
Christies, *(use of their reproduction of the title page picture)*
English Heritage, *42, 47–50, 54, 60, 83*
Foster Associates, *84*
Greater London Record Office, *5, 19, 22, 34, 38*
Guildhall Library, *55*
Hulton Picture Company, *45*
Illustrated London News Picture Library, *30, 56*
Institution of Civil Engineers, *57*
Peter Jackson, *14*
Andy Kemp, *86*
London Regeneration Consortium, *78, 81, 85*
National Monuments Record, *10*

National Portrait Gallery, *75*
National Railway Museum, *Jacket, 32, 36, 37, 40, 41, 44, 53, 61, 64, 67, 77*
Public Record Office, *43*
Publifoto, *82*
Mark Puddy, *half-title*
RIBA Drawings Collection, *46*
Andrew Testa, *23*
Malcolm Tucker, *69*
Weintraub Screen Entertainments (from a still supplied by the British Film Institute), *21*
Christopher Wood, *(for permission to use the picture on the title pages)*
John Yates, *63, 65, 71*
Zoological Society of London, *20*

All the other illustrations have been supplied by the authors and publisher.

The cover illustration is of King's Cross Station when newly completed in 1852, its frontage uncluttered by forecourt buildings.

The half-title picture is present-day King's Cross epitomised. Camley Street Natural Park is set against a backdrop of gasholders and the tower of King's Cross station. (Photo: Mark Puddy)

The illustration on the title pages is from an oil painting by George Earl in 1893, entitled *Going North, King's Cross Station*. It is reproduced by kind permission of Christopher Wood esq and Messrs Christies.

First published 1990
by Historical Publications Ltd
32 Ellington Street, London N7 8PL
(Telephone 071–607 1628)

ISBN 0 948667 06 0

Typeset by Historical Publications Ltd
and Fakenham Photosetting Ltd
Printed in Great Britain by
Biddles Ltd, Guildford and Kings Lynn

Contents

Notes on Contributors

GORDON BIDDLE is a retired surveyor who for many years has studied industrial history, particularly waterways and railways. He helped to found the Railway & Canal Historical Society in 1954 and has written numerous articles and books on canals and railway architecture. He is active in transport heritage conservation.

OLIVER CARTER is a Principal Architect working for Cumbria County Council. He has been very interested in railway history for many years, and has published articles in journals including *The Architectural Review*. His book, *An Illustrated History of British Railway Hotels 1838–1983* (1990), tells the story of the railways' 145-year involvement in hotels.

STEPHEN DUCKWORTH is an industrial archaeologist and geographer. After graduating from the Ironbridge Institute he is now a vernacular buildings surveyor for the National Trust in Dorset.

ALAN FAULKNER is a Corporate Banking Manager with Midland Bank plc in Colchester. In his spare time he has written a series of books and articles about individual canals and various canal carrying companies. The list includes *The Grand Junction Canal*, published in 1972, and *The Warwick Canals* (1985).

MICHAEL HUNTER is Reader in History at Birkbeck College, University of London. He is the author of various books and articles on the history of ideas in the seventeenth century. He has also long been concerned with the study and preservation of London's historic heritage, and has published *The Victorian Villas of Hackney* (1981). He currently chairs the King's Cross Conservation Areas Advisory Committee.

BARRY JONES took a first degree in fine art before studying industrial archaeology at the Ironbridge Institute. He is now supervising the National Trust's vernacular buildings survey in the Chiltern Region.

GAVIN STAMP is an architectural historian and writer who does not drive and only travels by train, which is one reason why, since 1982, he has lived in a Georgian house in the heart of King's Cross with his wife Alexandra Artley. He is a long standing member of the Victorian Society and is Chairman of the Thirties Society. His books include *The Changing Metropolis*, a collection of the earliest photographs of London, and a history of *Telephone Boxes*.

ROBERT THORNE taught for Stanford University before joining the GLC Historic Buildings Division (subsequently the London Division of English Heritage). He now works for Alan Baxter & Associates, structural engineers. He is the author of a number of books and articles on nineteenth century industrial and commercial buildings, including *Liverpool Street Station* (1978), and *Covent Garden Market, its History and Restoration* (1980). While at English Heritage he carried out historical research and survey work on the King's Cross area, some of the results of which are incorporated in this book.

Preface

London is entering the 1990s bereft of many of the civic virtues that signify a great city. Though it has seldom attracted the same popular pride as foreign capitals like Paris and Vienna, it has until recently maintained a reputation for being a practical and comfortable place to live and work. What it has lacked in outward splendour it has made up for by being well-serviced, comparatively well-run and full of modest pleasures. It is these once distinct qualities which now seem to be rapidly disappearing, leaving no obvious substitutes in their place. The public transport system, once marvelled at by foreigners, has become tawdry and exasperating; affordable housing is almost impossible to find; and the city's public realm – its streets, open spaces and civic buildings – is falling into disrepair. Above all, there seems to exist no coherent strategy for the revival of London through the application of appropriate solutions to these problems.

The clearest innovation in strategic thinking in recent years has been in the shift of civic responsibilities from local government to the private sector. Developers have been persuaded to provide public amenities and services of a kind which traditionally have been municipal concerns. They are even becoming involved in the construction of new transport systems. In such cases the benefits produced are nearly always tied to office developments, and because they are related to commercial projects of this kind they do not necessarily resolve wider metropolitan problems. On the contrary, some would argue that the dependence of public works on the expansion of the office sector has the effect of worsening existing conflicts and inequalities. Agreements to provide facilities by such means smooth the way for the over-production of offices at the expense of other priorities, while directing public improvements such as new railway lines away from places where they are most needed.

Such issues are well illustrated by what is at present occurring at King's Cross, which, today as throughout its history, is a model of what has happened to London. The current proposals for a massive development on the 134 acres of former railway land to the north of King's Cross station – for which a planning application is currently pending – highlight the question of how major urban developments should be paid for and who benefits most from them. Indeed, though the emphasis of this book is on what has gone on in this specific area in the recent and more distant past, the implications of this are broader: King's Cross needs to be seen in a wider metropolitan context in order to understand the full significance – both historical and contemporary – of developments there. We cannot single-handedly redress the unfortunate lack of civic vision which is besetting London, but we can hope to help widen the debate about the capital's future.

One thing that is inescapable about King's Cross and its adjoining area is the legacy that it represents of the impact on London of the great transport revolution of the nineteenth century. St Pancras and King's Cross, the London termini respectively of the Midland and Great Northern railways, are two of the finest railway stations in the world, triumphs of entrepreneurship and engineering skill. Their passengers were served by magnificent, purpose-built hotels, the Great Northern and the Midland Grand, both of which survive, though in contrasting condition and, currently, with contrasting prospects. To the north of the stations runs the Regent's Canal, the product of an earlier transformation in inland transport, while adjacent to this goods depots were established when the railways arrived, which took advantage of the proximity of the canal to organise the distribution of coal and other commodities to the metropolis. The King's Cross goods depot, dominated by its central feature, the Granary warehouse, survives miraculously intact, with almost all of the buildings erected there in the mid-Victorian period still standing: as such, it represents one of the most important industrial archaeological complexes in the country.

Equally inescapable is the far-reaching change that is about to take place. Work is about to begin on the restoration of the Midland Grand Hotel to its original magnificence: it is extraordinary that, after being in partial use as offices since it was closed as a hotel in 1935, this building has for years been standing completely empty. Meanwhile, the scheme currently proposed for the railway lands to the north threatens at least part of the former Goods Depot, which stands within the site, with destruction. In the immediate vicinity of King's Cross station, British Rail have plans for a London terminal for the Channel Tunnel, and, while the new station itself will be tunnelled under the King's Cross train-shed, an adjacent interchange building is planned which threatens the Great Northern Hotel with demolition. In addition, the construction of the lines into and out of the new station will necessitate large-scale demolition of buildings in adjacent parts of Islington and severe disruption further north. All in all, the area will within a few years be altered almost beyond recognition, and the question of what should survive of the old and how it should relate to the new is a critical one.

Debates about the future of the site, from whatever point of view, ought to be based on full information. Yet recent interest in the area has made it glaringly obvious that no book is currently available from which those anxious to learn more about its history can find out how King's Cross was originally developed, what operations were carried on there and about how the canal and railways and the activities associated with them affected the surrounding neighbourhood. It is to fill this gap that the present volume has been conceived. It stems from a one-day course on 'King's Cross and the Railway Age in London' held at Birkbeck College, University of London, on 26 November 1988, which comprised four illustrated talks on different aspects of the subject, together with a showing of *The Ladykillers* (1955): this Ealing Studios classic was filmed on location at King's Cross, and it formed an appropriate and entertaining conclusion to the day's proceedings.

Three of the chapters published here – Gavin Stamp's on the impact of change on the neighbourhood since the eighteenth century, Gordon Biddle's on the making of the two great termini and Robert Thorne's on the coal trade – are based on talks given on that occasion. In addition, we have recruited other authors to complete and extend our coverage, with Alan Faulkner writing on the canal and Oliver Carter on the hotels. We have also been fortunate in being allowed to incorporate in the book a shortened version of the definitive inventory of buildings and other features of industrial archaeological interest on the site compiled for English Heritage in autumn 1988 by Steve Duckworth and Barry Jones; they have also collaborated with Robert Thorne in writing an essay on the goods yard. Lastly, Michael Hunter, who organised the course at Birkbeck College, has contributed an account of recent developments in the area. This is necessarily somewhat provisional, since negotiations over the plans for the site will still be in progress when the book appears. But it should help to raise some of the broader issues concerning the future of the area which have already been alluded to, and which need to be fully discussed before it is too late.

We are grateful to the following for their assistance. Malcolm Tucker gave a talk at the Birkbeck course on 26 November 1988, and, although unfortunately unable to contribute a chapter to the book, he has been invaluable in placing his expertise at our disposal. The following have also contributed in different ways: Roy Burrows, Reg Ellis, Michael Ford, Charles Hadfield, Patrick Hannay, Ian Haywood, Phil Jeffries, Marion Kamlish, Randal Keynes, Robin Linsley, Bruce Methven, Jack Simmons, Teresa Sladen, Ann Swain, David Sulkin and John Yates.

Michael Hunter
Robert Thorne
July 1990

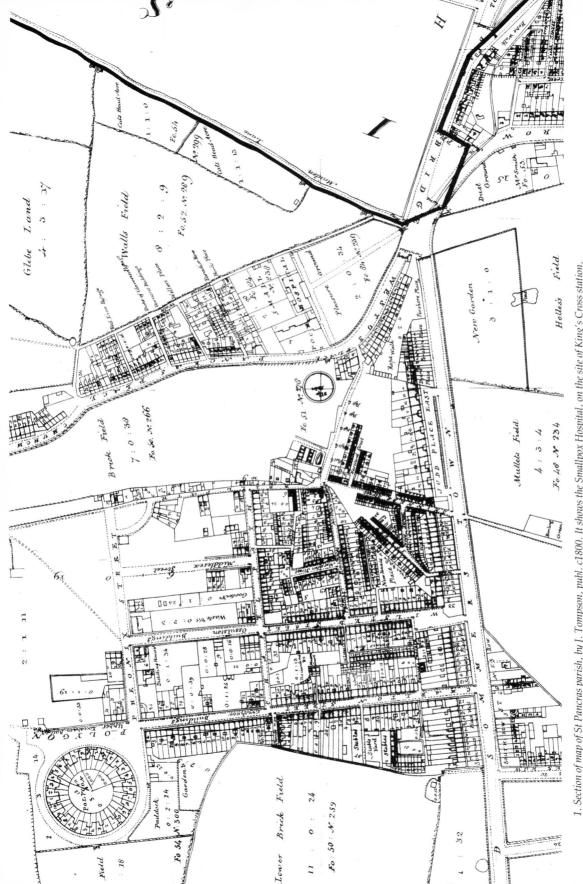

1. Section of map of St Pancras parish, by J. Tompson, publ. c1800. It shows the Smallpox Hospital, on the site of King's Cross station, lying back from the main road and behind it the tiny alleys which are still a feature of the station's hinterland. As will be seen to the left, St Pancras station replaced a maze of small dwellings.

CHAPTER ONE

From Battle Bridge to King's Cross: Urban Fabric and Change

Gavin Stamp

If the Great Northern Railway had not chosen to name its metropolitan terminus after a short-lived structure demolished a year before the company obtained its Act of Parliament, railway travellers on the East Coast main line would now arrive at 'London Battle Bridge'. The 'King's Cross' was a sort of memorial erected on the site of a turnpike at the important road junction where the New Road from Paddington to the City met the ancient Maiden Lane and the old road from Gray's Inn towards Hampstead. Designed by Stephen Geary, best known as the architect of Highgate Cemetery, it was intended to consist of a statue of the late King George IV, supported by the patron saints of England, Scotland, Wales and Ireland raised high above a Greek Doric base. Proposed in 1830 and completed by 1836, and apparently paid for by public subscription, this strange sixty-foot high structure suffered a decline as dramatic as that of poor Prinny's own reputation. The King was taken down in 1842 while the basement room, which had served successively as a police station, an exhibition room with a *camera obscura*, and a beer-shop, was demolished three years later.

Yet King's Cross survives as a name, despite the greater romance that attaches to 'Battle Bridge', the ancient crossing of the Fleet River by the Gray's Inn Road. Often supposed to commemorate an imaginary battle between Queen Boadiccea and the Roman invaders, or possibly a victory over the Danes by King Alfred, the name in fact is a corruption of 'Bradford Bridge' which itself was derived from 'Broad Ford'. In the reign of George III and, above all, in those of his sons, George IV and William IV, this important road junction was swallowed up by the Great Wen. Terraces and, occasionally, squares of standard, spec-built houses rapidly covered the surrounding farms and brickfields. And, despite the devastating impact of first the Regent Canal and then of the Victorian railway system, King's Cross remains a remarkably intact part of Georgian London, with greater interest given to the dense urban fabric by Victorian additions and rebuildings and not too much damage done – yet – by redevelopment since the Second World War.

Although populous and central, King's Cross remains an area which is little known and whose history is not yet fully investigated. The story of the Georgian development of the part of King's Cross that lies in the old Borough of St Pancras was exhaustively researched in volume xxiv of the *Survey of London*, but this admirable volume tells little of the Victorian history of the area,

2. *The King's Cross statue being demolished in 1845.*

while the part of King's Cross that lies in the Borough of Islington (Battle Bridge lies precisely on the boundary) has yet to be properly explored by architectural and urban historians. Hence this attempt at a general portrait of a peculiarly rich and complex part of inner London which may well look very different in a few years' time.

Until the middle of the 18th century, the area now loosely described as King's Cross consisted largely of open fields but it also contained one of the most venerable buildings in London. Since its enlargement and ruthless 'restoration' by the architect A.D. Gough in 1847–48, Old St Pancras church has exhibited little of its medieval fabric but it is likely that it stands on one of the earliest Christian sites in the country. The church building was not mentioned in the *Domesday Book* but the area was already known as 'St Pancras'. This dedication to Pancratius, the Roman saint martyred in about the year 304, is unusual and tradition insists, reinforced by the archaeological evidence of Roman occupation in the area, that a Christian church was founded here on the site of a Pagan temple possibly as early as the 4th century.[1]

Other early buildings in the area were inns, such as the Brill in Somers Town and the Pindar of Wakefield and the Boot off Gray's Inn Road. The latter was illustrated in Charles Dickens' *Barnaby Rudge* as the meeting place for the

3. Old St Pancras Church, 1815, before its restoration in 1847–48.

fomenters of the Gordon Riots. The name survives on the Victorian pub built on the site in Cromer Street, as did, until recently, the famous and ancient name of the 'Pindar' in the Gray's Inn Road on the 19th century building now fatuously renamed as The Water Rats. There were also other places of entertainment in the area, notably Chad's Well and Bagnigge Wells, both of which long extinct spas lay in the irregular triangle formed by the Gray's Inn Road and King's Cross Road.

Change began in 1756 when the 'New Road from Paddington to Islington' was laid out by Act of Parliament. A straight stretch, now the Euston Road, led from Tottenham Court Road to Battle Bridge where the alignment shifted southwards to run up to the Angel – now the Pentonville Road. The Act stipulated that no buildings were to be erected on new foundations within fifty feet of the new road, with the result that, for the first century of its existence, the New Road was wholly residential in character and lined by long gardens in front of the houses. Some public buildings were also erected along this great artery, notably St Pancras New Church, the magnificent Greek Revival building by the Inwoods erected in 1819–22 on the south-east corner of Euston Square. There was also the Smallpox Hospital which was moved from Windmill Street, Tottenham Court Road, to gardens immediately to the north of Battle Bridge in 1767. The hospital was rebuilt in 1793–94 with a cupola and in 1802 it was joined on its western side by the separate Fever Hospital. Both buildings were demolished after they were purchased in 1846 by the Great Northern Railway to make way for its terminus.[2]

Perhaps owing to the proximity of the Smallpox Hospital but more likely because it had become a major road junction, Battle Bridge failed to become as salubrious as the western stretches of the New Road. By the early 19th century

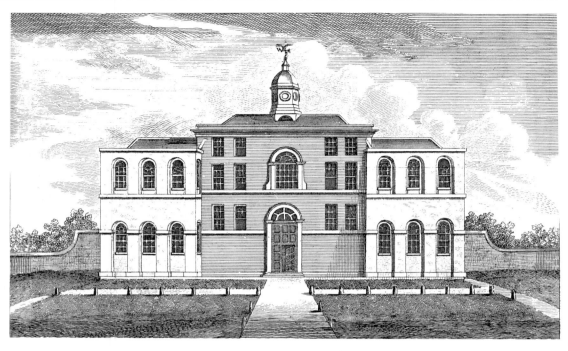

4. The Smallpox Hospital at King's Cross, demolished by the Great Northern Railway in 1846.

the area was conspicuous for brickfields and dust heaps. These brickfields of Somers Town and elsewhere were needed for the rapid urbanisation of the area which occurred after the end of the Napoleonic Wars, while a huge heap of ashes, collected for mixing with brick earth, stood on the corner of the Gray's Inn Road, directly opposite the Hospital. It was removed in 1826 to make way for houses – the material, according to preposterous legend, being shipped to Russia to make bricks for the rebuilding of Moscow.

In 1742–47 Thomas Coram's Foundling Hospital had been built in its grounds about half a mile to the south of Battle Bridge, and over the next eighty years the intervening space was gradually built over. The first significant developments were, however, close to Battle Bridge. The apex of that tongue of land formed by the junction of what are now the Gray's Inn Road and King's Cross Road was built up with small houses in the two decades after 1767 and more houses were built on the land behind the Smallpox Hospital by the end of the century. These have all now disappeared, as have almost all of the rather better class of houses erected in Somers Town at about the same time.

Somers Town lay on land owned by Sir Charles Cocks, Bart., who was created Baron Somers of Evesham in 1784. The developer was Jacob Leroux who, according to the *Gentleman's Magazine* in 1813, 'built a handsome house for himself, and various streets were named from the title of that noble Lord, a chapel was opened, a polygon begun in a large square, and every thing seemed to proceed prosperously, when some unforeseen cause occurred, which checked the fervour of building, and many carcases of houses were sold for less than the value of the materials'.[3] The most interesting part of the development was this Polygon, originally an isolated circle of 32 semi-detached four-storey houses built by Job Hoare for Leroux in 1793–92. William Godwin, the political reformer, took a flat in one of these houses in 1797 on his marriage to Mary Wollstonecraft, who died there in the same year after giving birth to the future Mary Shelley.

5. Smith's dust heap at the end of Gray's Inn Road.

6. The Roman Catholic church of St Aloysius, facing the semi-detached villas of the Polygon.

The Polygon was soon incorporated into Clarendon Square as the grid-plan of Leroux's development was laid out around it. Leroux built himself his handsome house on the north side of the square. This was subsequently occupied by the Abbé Carron, one of many refugees from the French Revolution who lodged in Somers Town because the area was cheap. For the benefit of his co-religionists, the Abbé in 1808 built the Roman Catholic Church of St Aloysius on the south side of the square, a handsome Classical chapel which was further embellished in 1850 by his successor, the Revd John Nerinckx. Most of Georgian Somers Town has disappeared in the cause of slum clearance, but there was no excuse whatever for the destruction of this elegant and early monument in the history of Roman Catholicism in London and its replacement by a mediocre modern structure in Eversholt Street in 1968. Fortunately, the Anglican Church of St Mary the Virgin in Eversholt Street survives. This starved essay in Gothic was built in 1824–27 and was satirised by Pugin in a plate in his *Contrasts* of 1836. The architects were W. & H.W. Inwood, the architects of St Pancras New church, whose much greater accomplishment in neo-Greek was further confirmed in two other churches of the 1820s: All Saints', Camden Street, and St Peter's, Regent Square, whose portico and steeple, having survived the Blitz, were gratuitously destroyed by the Diocese of London in the 1960s.

Pentonville, to the east of Somers Town on the other side of the Fleet in the Parish of St James, Clerkenwell, was another early development. The land belonged to Henry Penton, M.P. for Winchester, who exploited the salubrious

7. *St Mary the Virgin, Eversholt Street, as depicted in Pugin's* Contrasts.

and convenient situation of the heights of Islington just north of the New Road. The first houses were built in 1773 in Penton Street and in what is now the Pentonville Road and by the end of the century development extended down the hill towards, but not as far as, Battle Bridge. St James's Chapel, whose pretty Adamesque facade appears in the foreground of O'Connor's painting of *St Pancras at Sunset*, was built in 1787–88 and designed by Aaron Henry Hurst. It had been first proposed in 1777 by Penton to benefit his estate but difficulties with the incumbent of St James's, Clerkenwell, postponed its consecration until 1791. The building was modified in 1933 and, after several years of scandalous neglect, was demolished in 1984. Grimaldi, the famous clown who lived in Penton Place and Penton Street, is buried in the churchyard.

The area south of the New Road and north of Bloomsbury developed slightly later. Brunswick Square next to the Foundling Hospital was built by James Burton in 1792 and Mecklenburgh Square followed soon after, but Regent Square was not built up until 1829. The houses in Harrison Street were erected a decade earlier. Both lay on the Harrison Estate and it was the Harrisons who had accumulated the huge heap of ashes at Battle Bridge for brick making. Next to the north was Lucas Street, now Cromer Street, on the Lucas Estate, which was built up with houses between 1801 and 1815. Some were built by James Burton, who was to become Nash's favourite builder, but almost all of these have now disappeared. A little further to the north-west was the land owned by the Skinners' Company which extended over the New Road. Much of this was developed by James Burton. Burton Street was built up in 1809–20 and Cartwright Gardens, originally Burton Crescent, dates from the same period. These houses were of a higher quality than many in the Battle Bridge area, as are the surviving four storey houses in Judd Street, built between 1808 and 1816. Thanet Street, behind Judd Street, is interesting as a street of handsome

8. St James's Chapel, Pentonville Road, c1787.

9. No. 62 Tonbridge Street, photographed prior to the tunnelling of an underground line beneath the street.

two-storey workmen's cottages, built in 1812–22. The Skinners' Estate extended further east to Tonbridge Street, but the little Regency houses here were all swept away for slum clearance early this century. Most fortunately, their appearance, together with that of Judd, Leigh and Marchmont Streets, was recorded in a magnificent series of photographs taken in 1903 for use as evidence in any claims for damage provoked by the building of the tunnels beneath for the Great Northern, Piccadilly and Brompton Railway (the Piccadilly line).[4]

Houses of greater architectural pretension are still to be found further east in Frederick Street on the Calthorpe Estate. In 1814 Lord Calthorpe applied for an Act to pave streets on his estate between the Gray's Inn Road and the Fleet, and in 1823 he leased the northern part to the great builder Thomas Cubitt, who had established his works in the Gray's Inn Road shortly before. Cubitt began building houses in Frederick Street in 1826 and the terraces here seem to have been intended as something of a showpiece, differing in subtle details from the standard Late Georgian type. Some are of brick, some have plaster pilasters and some are entirely faced in painted stucco. The finest are the three four-storey houses facing down Frederick (now Ampton) Place: stuccoed, with ornamental parapets, they boast elegant iron roofed balconies to the unusually large windows of the first floor and segment-headed windows above.[5] Further north, on land sold to James Swinton in 1773, Swinton and Acton Streets were built up soon after at their western ends, but the remainder of these streets sloping down to the Fleet were not lined with houses until the 1830s and 1840s.

Curiously, the last parts of Battle Bridge to be developed were the areas immediately to the south-west and north-east of King's Cross itself. This was no doubt owing to the unsavoury reputation of the area – 'a haunt of thieves and murderers'[6] – as well as the proximity of dust heaps, brick fields and the Smallpox Hospital and to the often flooded banks of the River Fleet. Changing the name from Battle Bridge to King's Cross was a developer's ploy to improve the image of the area, rather like estate agents referring to 'West Kensington' or 'South Chelsea' rather than Hammersmith and Battersea. W. Forrester Bray, builder of the first houses on the Battle Bridge Estate, toyed with calling the area 'Boadiccea's Cross' or 'St. George's Cross' until the advent of the free-standing structure at the road junction bearing the statue of George IV provided a name with Royal cachet. The King's Cross was ridiculed by Cruikshank and satirised by Pugin in *Contrasts* by unfavourable comparison with the Market Cross at Chichester. Contemporary prints suggest that this unusual monument was not as unsightly as is always suggested, but the Vestry ordered its demolition as a public nuisance in 1845.[7] So passed the eponymous glory of King's Cross – but the name stuck.

Messrs Dunston, Robinson and Flanders, owners of the land immediately south of Battle Bridge and of a strip on the north side of the New Road, applied for an Act to develop in 1824. The first houses in Chesterfield (now Crestfield) Street, and Liverpool (now Birkenhead) Street, were built by Bray in 1825 and the first houses in Manchester (now Argyle) Street, date from 1826. That was the year the great dust heap on the corner of the Gray's Inn Road was removed and the first houses in Derby (now St Chad's) Street, were completed the following year. All these houses are of the standardised Late Georgian 'Third Class' (according to the Building Act of 1774) which make up so much of central London. That is, they are two bays wide with three storeys and a basement and have a single arched window on the ground floor and two tall windows on the *piano nobile*. Although plain and severe, these houses always had a carefully designed front door and case with a fanlight of elegant design above and ornamental cast-iron balconies on the first floor. Writing of the slightly later houses in Belgrove Street, the *Survey of London* notes that, 'Although the houses are narrow, rarely exceeding 16 feet wide, and can only have been intended for tenants of moderate means, they exhibit considerable ingenuity in design. All the detail is admirably executed and they have a marked dignity of composition.'[8]

As the *Survey* also comments, it is interesting to find that a development of 'third class' houses still included a square, but this was partly owing to the collapse of an ambitious project intended to increase the attractiveness of the area. This was the Panharmonium Gardens promoted by Signor Gesualdo Lanza, an Italian music teacher, who proposed a Grand Panharmonium Theatre with ballroom and refreshment rooms to stand in pleasure grounds south of the New Road. Plans were drawn up by Stephen Geary, architect of the King's Cross, but only a little theatre in Birkenhead Street seems to have been built. The Royal Panharmonium Gardens opened in 1830. The attractions included a 'Suspension Rail-Way' or 'monorail' but although an illustration was published showing the elaborate 'William the Fourth, Royal Car' suspended beneath the rail, it is not clear if this curious anticipation of the subsequent history of King's Cross was ever in operation. Like the King's Cross itself, the Gardens were a flop and within two years the land was divided up for building. Argyle Square was laid out over the gardens. Most of the houses here date from the 1840s and differ from those in the surrounding streets by being of four storeys and having architraves to the first-floor windows.

The disappearance long ago of yet another unusual building in King's Cross must be regretted. The London Horse and Carriage Repository ran behind and

10. *Argyle Square at peace with itself in 1949.*

11. *The London Horse and Carriage Repository, Gray's Inn Road.*

12. Keystone Crescent as seen today.

parallel to the Gray's Inn Road between St Chad's Street and Argyle Street. It was a structure of some architectural pretension with a large courtyard whose early history is remarkable. Robert Owen took over the place in 1832 as the home of his 'Equitable Labour Exchange' or 'Bazaar'. In the same year, Edward Irving brought his Irvingite congregation here after he had been expelled from his Scottish Church in Regent Square – the now destroyed miniature York Minster designed by William Tite – but disliked the association with the social reformer. After both Owen and Irving had departed, Madame Tussaud exhibited her waxworks in the building from 1833 until 1835. Subsequently the site was used for Whitbread's bottling plant and is today a garage. All traces of the original building have disappeared, including the Ionic portico which marked the entry from No. 277 Gray's Inn Road, which was still standing in 1952.[9]

Development of the opposite side of Battle Bridge, within the corner bounded by Maiden Lane and the Pentonville Road, was undertaken at about the same time and assisted by the laying out of the Caledonian Road. This new road was the result of an Act of Parliament of 1825 obtained by the Battle Bridge and Holloway Road Company. The long straight stretch south of the bridge over the Regent Canal was aligned directly towards the turnpike that would be replaced by the King's Cross but, in the event, the final hundred or so yards of the new road deviated southwards, presumably so as to create more convenient building plots as well as avoiding further traffic congestion at the Battle Bridge junction where five major thoroughfares already met. Houses soon lined the southern end of the Caledonian Road while the new 'Model Prison', now the Pentonville Prison, was built next to its northern extremity in 1840.

A particular delight of the Caledonian Road is the tiny Keystone Crescent (originally Caledonian Crescent) tucked behind the bend near King's Cross. This tight curve of tiny Fourth Rate houses was first occupied in 1846, the date that also appears on the arch in the western side of the terraces in Balfe (formerly Albion) Street, leading through to a 'Works' (Albion Yard), for manufacturing washing blue and black lead, established over a decade earlier, in 1832, on a green field site. Houses of greater pretension were erected in 1842 a little further east in North (now Northdown) Street, where four four-storey houses were given giant stuccoed pilasters to support a raised brick pediment as a centrepiece to close the vista down Collier Street. From this point, the urban development of King's Cross became contiguous with that of Pentonville.

In 1850 the North London Railway, or more correctly, the East & West India Docks & Birmingham Junction Railway, crossed the Caledonian Road just south of the Model Prison on its journey from Bow and Islington to Chalk Farm and this line now forms the effective northern boundary of the King's Cross area. By the end of the 1850s, the steady expansion of the built-up area had reached this railway, with the Early Victorian terraced houses and villas only differing from Late Georgian models in richer detailing and architraves to the windows. On the eastern side, small houses grew up along the Caledonian Road with more expensive property built on the higher areas of Barnsbury. On the western side, the terraces and squares of Somers Town continued on a grid northwards to Camden Town. But in between, east of the Regent Canal and west of Maiden Lane, there remained a great void on the map which was only briefly occupied by a development of houses. This was Agar Town, a name which has now disappeared but which, for the early Victorians, was a byword for urban squalor and disease.

In 1810, Counsellor William Agar purchased the lease of a mansion and grounds near Camden Town from the Prebend of St Pancras and built himself a smart new house, called Elm Lodge. In about 1840, following Agar's death, the southern part of the grounds were sold off by his widow on 21-year leases to working men to build their own houses. The result was 'Hagar Town' or 'Ague Town' – a slum without water supply or proper drainage which lay across the Regent Canal from the King's Road, now St Pancras Way, and north-east of the Old Church and St Pancras Workhouse. The horror of this isolated and short-lived development was eloquently described in 1851 by W.M. Thomas in an article for Charles Dickens' *Household Words* entitled 'A Suburban Connemara': '…The place, in its present state, is a disgrace to the metropolis. It has sprung up in about ten years. Old haunts of dirt and misery, suffered to exist in times when the public paid no attention to such matters, are difficult to deal with; but this is a new evil, which only began to come into existence about the time when Mr Chadwick's Report first brought before the public a picture of the filthy homes and habits of the labouring classes, and of the frightful amount of crime and misery resulting therefrom. In Agar Town we have, within a short walk of the City – not a gas-light panorama of Irish misery, 'almost as good as being there,' but a perfect reproduction of one of the worst towns in Ireland. The land is well situated – being high for the most part – and therefore capable of good drainage; and although too great a proximity to the cinder-heaps might make it an objectionable site for a superior class of dwellings, no spot could be better adapted for the erection of small tenements for labouring men and mechanics…'[10]

The street names in Agar Town – Durham Street, Oxford Street, Winchester Street and Salisbury Crescent – indicated that the Ecclesiastical Commissioners were the ground landlords. The Rector of St Pancras had erected a church in the area which was replaced, in 1862–63, by the now destroyed church of St Thomas, Wrotham Road (by S.S. Teulon) to the north, built at the expense of the Midland Railway. This was because the slums of Agar Town were not dealt with by either the Ecclesiastical or the Sanitary Commissioners but by the needs of the expanding railways, for both Agar Town and Elm Lodge were swept away by the Midland Railway, first for a coal depot, authorised in 1858 and completed in 1865, and then for the main line into St Pancras. The name of the (unfairly?) notorious Counsellor is now only commemorated by Agar Grove, formerly St Paul's Road, north of the North London Line.

Battle Bridge had an unsavoury reputation long before the importunate railways made their impact, although the destructive advent of the Great

Northern Railway's terminus and, above all, of the Midland Railway's station ensured that the area remained overcrowded, socially undesirable and characterised by a complex mixture of residential and industrial uses. The first railway to affect the area was the London and Birmingham (subsequently the London & North Western), which announced its arrival north of Euston Square with the great Doric propylaeum – the Euston arch – which was so wickedly destroyed in 1961–62. But the social aspirations of the developers of King's Cross had already been doomed by the building of the Regent's Canal. As Alan Faulkner explains in Chapter Two, an Act to build a canal from the Grand Junction Canal at Paddington to the River Thames at Limehouse, had been passed in 1812 and it opened in 1820. The route passed through Camden Town and then swung south towards Battle Bridge before turning east under Maiden Lane to disappear in a tunnel under Islington Hill. The provision of a basin east of Maiden Lane near Battle Bridge ensured that industrial enterprises would continue in the area while the erection of the premises of the Imperial Gas Company, authorised in 1822, on the south bank of the canal to the west of Maiden Lane effectively blighted the area north of the Smallpox Hospital.

This blight enabled the Great Northern Railway to reach its terminus at King's Cross with comparatively minor destruction of property, for there was little in its way – although for contemporaries, 'The destruction of property has been immense…At the present time [1851] there is nothing to be seen, from the New Road to the canal, but the sites of whole streets of destroyed houses, and the preparations for forming the permanent terminus.'[11] In 1846 a Royal Commission had recommended that no railway should penetrate central London beyond the New Road and the Great Northern's Act of the same year allowed the company to demolish the Smallpox Hospital in its grounds right by King's Cross and the small area of little houses just to the north – 'the awful rookery at the back of St Pancras Road'[12] – to build the simple arcuated stock brick station designed by Lewis Cubitt. From there, the line passed immediately east of the gasworks before plunging into the Gasworks Tunnel under the canal and Maiden lane, the ancient main road to the north. As 'bonestores, chemical works, and potteries render it peculiarly unsavoury',[13] Maiden Lane had few buildings along its winding length other than tile kilns and the land to its west as far as Agar Town was completely open. This was an ideal site for the Great Northern to build its goods yard, with direct and level access to the Regent Canal.

Future railway developments were not so well tailored to the existing fabric of London, however. Next came the Metropolitan Railway, the first underground line in the world, running from Paddington to Farringdon Street, on which work began in 1859. From Marylebone to King's Cross, the railway was built by 'cut and cover' under the Euston Road but beyond King's Cross it swung south to cut under the Fleet before tunnelling under Clerkenwell. This curve required the demolition of the buildings on the narrow tongue of land formed by the junction of the Gray's Inn and Pentonville Roads while the 'up' tunnel connecting with the Great Northern's main line along York Road, the new name for Maiden Lane, cut through property north of Pentonville Road. All these lines opened in 1863 and the success of the diversion of the Great Northern's suburban services to the City through these tunnels was such that in 1864 the Metropolitan Railway decided to increase its line through Clerkenwell from two to four tracks. These 'Widened Lines', opened in 1868, destroyed yet more of the little Georgian houses such as survived in the tangle of streets between the Gray's Inn and King's Cross Roads.

But the Midland Railway was far more destructive. Work began on building the new line into London in 1864 and the colossal terminus high above the Euston Road opened in 1868. The line passed under the North London Railway

13. Cut-and-cover tunnelling for the Metropolitan Railway at King's Cross, engraved for the Illustrated London News *in 1861.*

and then over the Regent's Canal just to the west of the Great Northern goods yard. It then passed through the St Pancras Burial Ground, which the company considered an easier and cheaper alternative to purchasing the gasworks. In the event this proved a troublesome and scandalous operation, with Thomas Hardy being involved in supervising the exhumation and reburial of closely packed decomposing bodies. But the damage to the living was even greater, for the railway not only wiped out the slums of Agar Town but also a sizeable chunk of Somers Town.

Nobody thought the replacement of Agar Town by the Midland Railway's goods yard anything but a public boon – 'If the Midland Railway had conferred no other benefit on London and Londoners, our thanks would be due to it for having cleared away the whole, or nearly the whole, of the above-mentioned miserable district of mud and hovels, and given us something better to look upon'[14] – for that was the conventional attitude to slum clearance, with little thought given to rehousing the dispossessed slum-dwellers. But building the St Pancras terminus required the removal of three thousand rather more substantial houses in seven streets in Somers Town. Even this was accepted with equanimity by John Hollingshead, the author of *Ragged London in 1861*: 'The whole of Somers Town…is a worthy neighbour of Agar Town. It is filled with courts and alleys…and is crowded with cheap china-shops, cheap clothiers, and cheap haberdashers. Its side streets have a smoky, worn-out appearance; the gas lamps project jauntily from the walls, the iron posts at the end lean towards each other as if for mutual support; every street door is open; no house is without patched windows; and every passage is full of children. Back views of dingy public-houses make the scene more dismal; and wherever there is a butcher's shop it contrives to look like a cat's meat warehouse. Chapel Street is the chief centre of business...[15]

Chapel Street would be largely obliterated by the Midland Railway's compulsory clearances.'It will, perhaps, be said that in the long run the vicinity has benefitted in every way; but it is to be feared that in the process of improvement the weakest have been thrust rather rudely to the wall.'[16] This was all too true: the railways were not at first obliged to rehouse displaced tenants and evaded their responsibilities when they eventually were. The ground landlords in Somers Town were paid by the Midland Railway but their unfortunate tenants received not a penny of compensation, despite taking their case to the Bloomsbury County Court in 1865 (The judge 'felt the hardship of the tenants' case, and expressed his regret at the decision he was compelled to arrive at.'[17]) Another casualty was the church of St Luke on the Euston Road, but in this case the railway paid for a new church: St Luke's, Oseney Crescent in Kentish Town (designed by Basil Champneys rather than J. Johnson, the architect of the destroyed building).

In 1874 the Midland Railway sought powers for further expropriation, but its behaviour in the previous decade had caused such ill-feeling that the proposal to sweep away the rest of St Pancras Churchyard and the Old Church was stoutly resisted. The company did, however, secure permission to acquire a further 14 acres of Somers Town – a larger area than had been needed for the terminus – to build a goods station on the Euston Road. 10,000 people were apparently to be displaced: a figure which seems very high but may well have included many of the unfortunates already evicted for the station and who had then added to the desperate overcrowding in the area. The *Builder* considered that, 'a visit to the spot would be sufficient to convince the most sceptical that a more dilapidated or disease-ridden block of hovels does not exist in any part of the metropolis',[18] but one man's hovel is another man's home – and posterity's listed building. In this case however, the Midland Railway did enter into an agreement with the Metropolitan Artizans Dwelling Company to build workers' tenements elsewhere for some of those displaced. The houses were cleared in 1878. Work did not begin on the goods station until 1883 and the building with its magnificent red-brick Gothic arcaded walls was finished in 1887. Damaged in the Second World War, it is now the site of the British Library.

The hugely destructive railway works of the 1860s did, fortunately, have architectural compensations. The buildings on the acute road junction facing King's Cross, destroyed to build the Metropolitan Railway, were replaced by a suitable new block with a 'lighthouse' tower above the curved corner in about 1875. Buildings in a similar Italianate style, larger and more elaborately detailed than the surrounding Georgian terraces, also rose on the north side of the Pentonville Road. The Bell public house, a florid Classical gin palace, also rose on the south side of the same road next to the Metropolitan Station (now the Thameslink Station), while the east side of York Road became lined with a mixture of houses, pubs and light industrial buildings of the 1850s and 1860s. Another comprehensive rebuilding occurred along the west side of Pancras Road when the building of the station in the 1860s required a regularisation of the old road. The curve of the Great Northern Hotel, built in 1851, reflects the old alignment of what was called Weston Place (the opposite side of which was removed in 1871.[19] Further north, new brick buildings in an eclectic style replaced what remained of the Georgian slums around Paradise Row. Pubs, shops and Stanley Buildings – erected by the Improved Industrial Dwelling Company in 1864–65 – line the road opposite Gilbert Scott's Gothic arcaded

14. *King's Cross at the height of the horse-drawn era, watched over by the 'lighthouse building'.*

15. *(Opposite) the German Gymnasium in action, 1866. Climbing ropes hang from the roof trusses.*

16. *(Opposite) 'St Pancras Hotel and Station from Pentonville Road: Sunset' (1881), by John O'Connor.*

station wall, but the most interesting building lies tucked behind and is announced on the Pancras Road frontage only by the cryptic legend 'Turnhalle' above an arched entrance. This is the gymnasium for the German Gymnastic Society designed by Edward Grüning and built, again, in 1864–65. It is remarkable for retaining roof trusses of laminated timber of the sort which once covered the two train sheds of King's Cross station.

When John O'Connor painted his *St Pancras at Sunset* in 1884, the railways had done their worst. With the completion of the Somers Town goods station, no large scale changes would take place in the heart of King's Cross for a century. The building of what are now the Piccadilly Line and the City branch of the Northern Line in the early years of this century made hardly any impact above ground (only the now disused station in York Way, in Leslie Green's typical style faced with ruby-red tiles, testifies to what goes on below ground). The same was true of the Victoria Line in the 1960s. O'Connor's view down the Pentonville Road has, understandably, become the quintessential image of the Victorian city. Rows of shabby, densely packed and much used Georgian terraces are broken by the occasional chapel and Victorian commercial building while in the distance loom those massive symbols of industrial power, the two great mid-Victorian termini. It is a scene of smoke and dirt, bustle and confusion, continuity and progress.

Whether such a view, such an urban concentration, seems appalling or attractive is a subjective matter. There are many quotations referring to slums

and rookeries in the King's Cross area but clearly it was also a vital and vigorous part of London, one not depressed or uniformly poverty-stricken by any means. The presence of railway stations often generated poverty – as much through displacement of residents as because smoke and noise were undesirable neighbours – while the presence of small but smelly industrial workshops further militated against it being a respectable residential area. Fortunately we have a document which gives an objective picture of the social complexity of King's Cross in the 19th century both to underpin and to contradict the many subjective descriptions of urban squalor. This is Charles Booth's *Descriptive Map of London Poverty 1889* which, by coloured overprinting, reveals the result of a scientific survey conducted in the late 1880s as part of his great work *Life and Labour of the People in London.*

Booth's top category, 'Upper-middle and Upper classes. Wealthy.' was represented on the map by yellow. The nearest this appears to King's Cross is Tavistock Square and Endsleigh Gardens but there is a certain amount of red – 'Well-to-do. Middle class.' – along the south side of the Euston Road, around Argyle Square, around Oakley Square in Camden Town and Thornhill Square in Barnsbury and even a splash of red in Pancras Road and York Road. It is surprising to find the old Battle Bridge Estate in this colour, as in 1848 a report on destitute districts wrote of 'an extensive field of labour situated between Cromer Street and the New Road on one side, and Judd Street and Gray's Inn Road on the other' where five families could share a house, drunkenness and squalor were prevalent, and most people were labourers, beggars and street traders. But by 1907 Argyle Square could be described as 'chiefly composed of 'apartments' and small private hotels.'[20] Perhaps the advent of the railway terminii had actually improved this particular area.

Most of the King's Cross area on Booth's map is, however, a complicated patchwork of pink, mauve and light-blue. Pink was 'Fairly comfortable. Good ordinary earnings'. Mauve was 'Mixed. Some comfortable, others poor' and light-blue represented 'Poor. 18s. to 21s. a week for a moderate family.' The Polygon was mauve, as was Cartwright Gardens, Cromer Street, Britannia Street and the area around the Islington canal tunnel. A deep blue, for 'Very poor, casual. Chronic want.' appeared in pockets behind better class streets, such as in parts of Somers Town and off the lower Caledonian Road. Worst of all was purple, the 'Lowest Class. Vicious, semi-criminal.' Large blocks of this colour fall between the little streets north of Cromer Street, in parts of Somers Town north of Clarendon Square and in isolated pockets near the Caledonian Road.

Consciousness of poverty and the dangers of disease in overcrowded urban areas made a considerable change to the Late Georgian urban fabric of King's Cross, for many examples of model working class housing were erected as slum clearances. Indeed, the very first model housing experiment was made near King's Cross when, in 1844–46, the newly founded Society for Improving the Condition of the Labouring Classes erected Model Buildings off Lower Road or Bagnigge Wells Road, now King's Cross Road, below Mount Pleasant. These were designed by Henry Roberts and were 'a double row of two-storey houses, facing each other, and on three distinct plans, to accommodate in the whole twenty-three families, and thirty single females'.[21] This was followed, in 1847, by the now destroyed Metropolitan Dwellings in Pancras Square, on the corner of Old Pancras Road and Platt Street, erected by the Metropolitan Association for Improving the Dwellings of the Industrious Classes.

Many examples of the typical working class tenement block of the 1860s and 1870s with open access balconies, often erected by the Improved Industrial Dwellings Company, can be found in the area. These include Stanley Buildings in Pancras Road and the several blocks in and around Britannia Street off King's Cross Road. Soon after Booth published his map, the long notorious

Greetings from KINGS CROSS

G. N. R. & Piccadilly Tube Stations.

Euston Music Hall.

St Pancras Town Hall.

St Pancras New Church.

Old Church, St Pancras.

slums just north of Cromer Street were dealt with by the East End Dwellings Company. Four large courtyard blocks of tenements were erected, one a year, beginning in 1891, and over the next two decades further blocks of flats replaced the small Georgian houses in Tonbridge Street and Hastings Street. All that now remains of the original urban fabric is the small (doomed) two-storey terrace in Argyle Walk.

Cromer Street had long been notorious for poverty and prostitution which is why, in 1888–89, Holy Cross Church was built in the middle of the long street then lined with shops and pubs. In his description of the work of this extreme Romanist Anglican parish, Charles Booth noted how, 'This corner of London …is cursed by the street-walking form of prostitution, for which many of the small hotels in the neighbourhood of the railway terminii offer facilities. The lowest of these women used to live in the vile quarter off Cromer Street, which has given way to model buildings and some still live near, but women come here from all parts…'[22] The Holy Cross church itself, which replaced an earlier temporary mission established in 1876, was designed by Joseph Peacock. Ian Nairn wrote of it in 1966 that, 'The outside is cheap and shrugged off; there are a hundred like it in London's suburbs. Inside it is as honest and selfless as King's Cross Station, which is only a few yards away. Nothing unnecessary, and nothing put on for form's sake as the big boys would have done. Narrow aisles, tall clerestory, high reaching-out east end. The church itself is worshipping…'[23]

The Church of England also had an important role to play in Somers Town. Fr Basil Jellicoe, vicar of St Mary's, Somers Town, was the moving force behind the foundation of the St Pancras House Improvement Society in 1924.'Somers Town', he wrote, ' is really gigantic theft. Overcrowding and poverty are here being used by the Devil in order to steal from the children of God the health and happiness which are their right.'[24] Housing improvements go back here to the late 19th century. The London County Council began the Churchway Estate of

17. An Edwardian souvenir of King's Cross. The Euston Music Hall (top right) stood on the site of the present town hall extension.

18. *Section of Stanford's map of London and its Suburbs, published in 1862. By now King's Cross station is in place, but the site of St Pancras station is still occupied by St Luke's church and the mean streets behind it.*

19. *The Ossulston Street Estate, built by the London County Council 1927–37.*

gently detailed blocks of red-brick flats in 1899 while the Midland Railway, atoning for its sins, erected the non-polygonal and now-destroyed Polygon Buildings in place of the Polygon in the centre of Clarendon Square in 1894. Slum clearance in Somers Town began in earnest in the 1920s. The LCC began building the large Ossulston Estate in 1927 and when it was completed a decade later 514 dwellings had been built stretching along the side of the Somers Town Goods Station in a series of polygonal courts. Stuccoed, with prominent arched entrances and a horizontal emphasis created by the open balconies, these flats may well have been influenced by contemporary housing in Vienna like the famous Karl-Marx-Hof. More typical of the usual LCC type of flats is Walker House further north, with brick facades organised in a careful neo-Georgian style.

20. Elephants being walked from the docks to the London Zoo.

The St Pancras House Improvement Society began with the reconditioning of eight houses in Gee Street and then began building blocks of flats. The first was St Mary's Flats in Drummond Crescent. These were followed by St Nicholas's and St Christopher's Flats and St Augustine's House in Werrington Street on the Sidney Estate in Sidney Street (purple on Booth's map), St George's and St Francis's Flats in Bridgeway Street, St Michael's Flats in Aldenham Street and St Anthony's Flats in Chalton Street. All were designed by Ian B. Hamilton in a sub-Georgian manner with prominent pantiled roofs, but what most distinguishes these buildings are the clothes' drying posts in the yards with their figurative and ornamental ceramic finials made by the sculptor Gilbert Bayes.[25]

The end result of all this rebuilding was to transform Somers Town from insanitary houses of two or three storeys with individual yards into an area of five or six storey blocks of flats with communal gardens. Yet this was done at a time when Continental observers like S.E. Rasmussen, the Danish author of *London: The Unique City*, were praising London for being a city of houses, not flats.'In England new slums largely develop in houses that have been given up by their middle-class owners. On the Continent we construct slums. You English must know that in all towns, in your own as well as others, there is a strong tendency to de-populate the most thickly populated areas. And this tendency is the right and wholesome one. But when replacing poor little houses by big blocks of flats, large sums are tied up in quarters which should normally de-populate, and wholesome evolution is thus hindered by the building of these large blocks. We on the continent know something of this, for we have learnt it to our cost. To build flats in slums will not stem the current,

London will continue to be a town of one-family houses, and it is tragic to see the enormous sums of money spent in this way and employed to a wrong purpose, for instead of planning the moving out of factories, business premises and private houses in connection with each other, living houses are being built with a quite un-English standard and according to types which are elsewhere recognized as inadequate.'[26] Time has only shown the wisdom of Rasmussen's remarks and it is sad that so many potentially charming terraces were swept away that today could be restored and lived in, like the similar houses in Keystone Crescent.

The twentieth century also left its mark on the public heart of King's Cross. Mediocre commercial buildings replaced most of the surviving Late Georgian houses which, with their long front gardens, once lined the Euston Road. Rather better is the St Pancras Town Hall opposite the Station, an essay in Portland stone by A.J. Thomas, which proclaims a deep debt to Lutyens, for whom the architect acted as office manager until 1935. Further to the east, the stuccoed Baroque facade of the King's Cross Cinema, now the Scala, rose up after King's Cross Bridge had been built over the Metropolitan Railway tunnel as an extension of Caledonian Road in 1910–12. The cinema also straddled the tracks and both works required the demolition of the station's original arched iron roof of 1862 (the Underground station itself was moved to the west in front of St Pancras Station in 1941). Designed by H. Courtenay Constantine, the cinema was eventually completed in 1921. Just a little to its south, the Willing Advertising building in Gray's Inn Road, with its statue of Mercury high above a pyramidal roof, is a particularly fine and eclectic Edwardian concoction of 1909 by Hart & Waterhouse. A final 20th century curiosity worthy of mention is Battle Bridge Flats on the corner of Goods Way and Battle Bridge Road. Of a mere two storeys nestling beneath the great Victorian gasholders, these were demonstration flats designed by John Gower and erected for the British Steel-work Association in 1936.

Given the prominence of the two railway terminii and their attendant goods yards in this part of central London, it is surprising that more damage was not caused by the Luftwaffe during the Blitz. (Ironically, in the Great War, a daylight raid in 1917 had managed to hit the German Gymnasium as well as St Pancras Station.) Houses rather than railway buildings were the principal casualties and, after the war, extensive bomb damage gave further impetus to the slum-clearance plans of the boroughs of St Pancras, Finsbury and Islington. Pentonville was transformed, as was the area east of York Way. The entire rebuilding of Cromer Street, begun in the 1930s, was continued immediately after the war by the erection of tall steel-framed blocks for railway workers by Hening & Chitty. The only other post-war flats of any architectural distinction are on the Priory Green Estate, north of the Pentonville Road, and Bevin House which replaced Holford Square, both being designed by Skinner, Bailey & Lubetkin. The former had been first proposed before the war for Finsbury Borough Council by Berthold Lubetkin, who, in 1942, had designed the short-lived monument to Lenin in Holford Square. Unfortunately, the most prominent modern building in the centre of King's Cross is the extension to the Town Hall which replaced the Euston Theatre in the 1960s.

However, despite bombing and slum clearance, King's Cross survived the war as a remarkably intact quarter of 19th-century London. This was, no doubt, the reason why it was chosen by Ealing Studios as an authentic Cockney location for the film *The Ladykillers*, released in 1955. Scenes were filmed in and outside King's Cross Station and in Vernon Rise off the King's Cross Road while the robbery itself took place outside Stanley Buildings in Cheney Road. The view from the front door of Mrs Wilberforce's house, the focus of the plot, was that from the Wardonia Hotel in Argyle Street, but the fanciful exterior of this curious Victorian reconstruction was erected at the end of Frederick Street,

21. Alec Guinness and Danny Green take their first victim to his fate: a still from The Ladykillers. *In the background are the tracks out of King's Cross and the North London line bridge.*

a cul-de-sac of Victorian tenements off the Caledonian Road due for redevelopment. From here, in the film, bodies were dropped into coal trucks at the entrance to the Copenhagen Tunnel on the main line out of King's Cross, a location which afforded a panoramic view of the North London Line viaduct and, beyond, of the smoke filled expanses of the King's Cross goods yard with the filigree outlines of the gasholders and the towers and spire of King's Cross and St Pancras terminating a strangely beautiful landscape of Victorian engineering, enterprise and ruthlessness. As Ian Nairn wrote in 1966, 'The whole of this place at the back of St Pancras is incredibly moving: tunnels, perspectives, trains on the skyline, roads going all ways. If you get nothing from it at first, stay there until something happens: it is really worth the effort.'[27]

Much has, of course, been lost in King's Cross which would have increased the architectural interest of the area. Churches, in particular, have suffered. In addition to the losses already mentioned, two others should be cited. That highly original essay in 'rogue' Gothic of 1863 by Joseph Peacock, St Jude's Church in Gray's Inn Road, was demolished in 1936, and the neo-Norman New Jerusalem Church, built in 1844 for the Swedenborgians on the south-east corner of Argyle Square, went in the war. But equally sad was the gratuitous destruction of a curious and charming stuccoed house in Cromer Street a little to the west of Holy Cross Church. This was the so-called 'Nell Gwynn's Cottage' or, more accurately, 'Compo Castle' as it had been elaborately faced in stucco ornaments. Set back from the street, it was demolished as an exercise in Air Raid Protection in 1938.[28]

No good new buildings have arisen to replace these interesting old ones, as can be seen in the King's Cross Road where the mediocre Ryan Hotel has replaced the terrace which was broken by steps ascending to Granville Square.

This was once the scene of urban decay that was closely observed by Arnold Bennett in *Riceyman Steps*, a novel published in 1923, which reveals the contemporary perception of down-at-heel Late Georgian London.[29] But it was not all shabbiness and decay: photographs of the interior of Reggiori's Restaurant, the turn-of-the-century conversion of that relic of the Panharmonium Gardens, the Royal Theatre in Birkenhead Street off the Euston Road, suggest that something fine has been lost, while the concrete Lilley & Skinner warehouse by Owen Williams of 1936–37 on the north side of the Pentonville Road has been replaced by a much less interesting building. Much of architectural distinction does survive, however, including some unexpected delights. Grand industrial buildings like the Granary were unknown until recently because inaccessible, but the real surprises in so apparently prosaic an area are interiors. Few would suspect the existence of a mid-Victorian Turkish Bath behind the drab Georgian exterior of No. 9 Caledonian Road while the interior of the Paget Memorial Hall, a mission in Randells Road, off York Way, in which that enigmatic Edwardian maverick, Beresford Pite, reused old Scottish woodwork, is the most extraordinary thing of its kind in London.

But the character and appeal of King's Cross does not depend upon individual buildings. The appeal is that of historic urban grain, of ordinariness and the typical, enhanced by peculiar topographical circumstances which generate dramatic contrasts. Not all find this attractive, it must be admitted. 'The general perception of the public,' asserts one commentator, 'is that these areas, apart from one or two obvious monuments such as the stations, are largely invisible and unknown, are dirty, run down and in need of redevelopment.' The same architect writes of the German Gymnasium that, 'few people other than workers and residents of the immediate vicinity penetrate this small area between

22. 'Nell Gwynn's Cottage' off Cromer Street, demolished in 1938.

Pancras Road and the railways. The roads and alleys around it are a remnant of the 19th century railway age, which, while interesting, convey a decayed (possible unsafe) feeling.'[30] Yet this is precisely the area that was used for the making of *High Hopes*, a recent film that ended with the view from the roof of Stanley Buildings and which saw the area not as decayed and hostile but attractive and full of hope and potential.

Anyone who loves London and really loves architecture can see through the grime and dereliction to what is underneath. King's Cross is the real stuff of which the capital is made. It is Georgian London, created in the last and stretched days of a civilized tradition of building. The stock bricks and painted stucco may now be cracked and dirty, but that is but patina, for the terraces have the charm of old friends who have declined gracefully with age and have,

23. Down and out in Pentonville Road, 1989. (Photo: Andrew Testa)

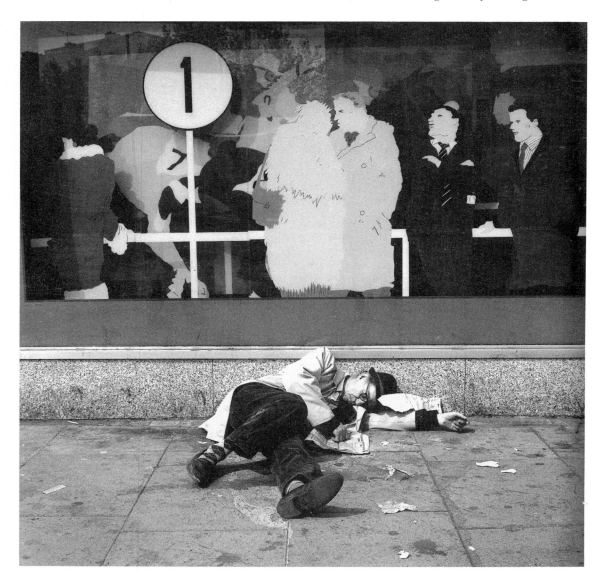

perhaps, fallen on hard times. Circumstances can always improve and all that is often needed is a little love and care. For King's Cross is more than just a chunk of Late Georgian London, enhanced and cut about by the more exuberant and more uneven architectural expressions of later generations. It has had a peculiar history both of failure and human degradation and of dramatic change. It is an area of unique topographical and social significance in the development of the capital and its busy, noisy streets provide a foil to some of the greatest monuments of industrial and transport history in the land. Monuments should not be seen in isolation. They arose in a particular context, and the context of the Victorian railway builders is the ordinary London of the early 19th century.

This is one reason why the protection of the fabric of King's Cross matters: to give that contrast in scale but continuity in urbanity which make the setting of King's Cross and St Pancras stations comprehensible and invigorating. Another reason is that many people are happy to live in the area. It is good that King's Cross is both a residential and a commercial area, for there is a growing consciousness that the 20th century planning insistence on 'zoning', on the separation of homes from places of work, has done much to destroy the vitality and character of cities. Now that noxious trades have disappeared, a dense mixture of residential, commercial and industrial uses can be seen as an advantage rather than a liability. As a result, King's Cross still has great vitality – and great potential as it stands. And, to a Londoner, this confused and largely unplanned area, characterised by human failure as well as enterprise, has its moments of real beauty – as the painter John O'Connor could see a century ago.

That great observer of London life, George R. Sims, wrote of King's Cross at the turn of the century: 'Stand at the corner opposite the Great Northern Railway side entrance, and if the proper study of mankind is man, you will have a great opportunity of pursuing a profitable course of education. Down Gray's Inn Road, Pentonville, Euston Road, and York Road flow endless streams of humanity, and the noise of the traffic is deafening, for here three great railway centres contribute their carrying trade to the general confusion. Travellers, especially provincial travellers, abound on the pavements, and the dialects and accents of all the counties of the United Kingdom mingle with the Cockney hubbub. It is here that the provincial newly arrived by rail is first faced with the problem of London's vastness. He wants to take a 'bus, but he doesn't know which 'bus to take… From dawn to midnight you will see a knot of loafers hanging about the King's Cross corner. If you are poetical and blessed with a strong imagination you may picture them as men who have been waiting year after year for friends from the provinces – friends who have never come. If you are matter-of-fact you will guess that the loafer loafs here because there are many opportunities of an odd copper, or a proffered drink…'[31]

That description might have been written today rather than in 1902. It is remarkable how little has changed in King's Cross, physically as well as socially – yet. In some ways that is depressing. Some change is certainly needed; much may come – but King's Cross has proved to be remarkably resilient. That is much of its 'appeal, which provides hope for the future.

FOOTNOTES

1   See Charles E. Lee, *St Pancras Church and Parish* (1955).
2   The history of these hospitals is confusing. The *Survey of London* states it moved to Battle Bridge in 1746, but that was before the New Road existed. Vol. vi of *London and its Environs Described* of 1761 states that the Smallpox and Vaccination Hospital was instituted in 1746 and was then in Cold Bath Fields. John Timbs' *Curiosities of London* (1867), agrees with this date and states that it was removed to Battle Bridge in 1767. The GNR paid for a new building at the foot of Highgate Hill while a new Fever Hospital was built in the Liverpool Road, Islington – see Knight's *Cyclopaedia of London*, (1851), 351.
3   Quoted in Vol. V of *Old and New London* by Edward Walford (c1880), 340.
4   These photographs, which were also taken for the building of the other lines promoted by the Underground Electric Railways Co. of London, Ltd., were inherited by London Transport and have since been distributed among the record offices of the appropriate London boroughs. Those of King's Cross are to be found in the Camden Public Library, Local History Collection, Swiss Cottage.
5   For Thomas Cubitt's works in the Gray's Inn Road and his development of the Calthorpe Estate, see Hermione Hobhouse, *Thomas Cubitt, Master Builder*, (1971).
6   Walter Thornbury, *Old and New London*, Vol. II (nd), 278.
7   Thornbury, *op.cit.*, 278. The *Survey of London* confirms that Bray built some of the houses on the Battle Bridge Estate. John Richardson in the Camden History Society *Newsletter*, No 61, Sep 1980, gives a full account of the history of the King's Cross and mentions that the original promoter was a Mr Guinette, who also had an interest in the Battle Bridge Estate. A view of the King's Cross, shorn of George IV – presumably to make the *camera obscura* – and the Saints, appears in C.F. Partington's *An Illustrated History of London* (1837), in which (204) it is described as an 'unsightly and unaptly-termed building...at present used as a police station.' Pugin's view, which is incorrect in topographical orientation, depicts the King in place but not the supporting Saints, which suggests that the Cross may never have been completed to the original design.
8   *Survey of London*, xxiv (1952), 108. The proper classification of this sort of house is slightly confusing as Peter Nicholson, in *The New and Improved Practical Builder and Workman's Companion* of 1823, illustrates a 'Third-Rate House' with four storeys and a basement and describes a three storey house with a typical King's Cross facade as 'Fourth-Rate', although his example has no basement. See Dan Cruickshank & Peter Wyld, *London: The Art of Georgian Building* (1975), 27.
9   That is, at the time of the preparation of the *Survey of London* volume, which reproduces one of the two views of the interior of the Repository published by Thomas Shepherd in *Metropolitan Improvements*, (1827). No architect's name is recorded in connection with the building.
10 W.M. Thomas, 'A Suburban Connemara' in *Household Words* no. 50 (8 Mar 1851), 562. Thomas gave a precise topographical description of the area, which is sometimes confused with the part of Somers Town much further south which also fell victim to the Midland Railway. The drawing of slums illustrated in *The Builder* in 1853 and reproduced in C.H. Denyer, ed., *St Pancras through the Centuries* (1935), 65A, under the title of 'Paradise Row, Agar Town' in fact shows Paradise Row which lay just to the west of King's Cross station, which can be seen in the background. Illustrations of the real Agar Town are given in the *Survey of London*, xix. A further contemporary description of Agar Town, after

a few imporvements and shortly before its extinction, is given by John Hollingshead in *Ragged London in 1861*, (1986).
11 *Knight's Cyclopaedia of London*, (1851), 846. The full description of King's Cross in 1851 is interesting: 'The site of the former Small-Pox Hospital is that chosen for the terminus of the Great Northern Railway. It is at the present time a vast wilderness, with the remains of razed houses strewn around. The destruction of property has been immense. In the first place the hospital, with the adjacent Fever Hospital, have been removed, and new structures built at the company's expense near Highgate. Then, all the houses which bounded those hospitals on the north have been removed to give an approach to the terminus; and, lastly, the whole of the property on the west side of Maiden Lane, from the New Road to the canal, has been razed to the ground, and the Lane itself doubled in width, to give a commodious road-approach to the goods station north of the canal. The buildings were all of a very humble character, except the hospitals, but the expense of purchase must nevertheless have been very large. We might hazard a conjecture that the northern [i.e. temporary] station...might have sufficed tolerably well both for passenger and goods traffic, and an expenditure of several hundred thousand pounds thereby saved; but the directors must be supposed to be the best judges of that matter. At the present time there is nothing to be seen, from the New Road to the canal, but the sites of whole streets of destroyed houses, and the preparations for forming the permanent terminus...'
12 J. Weale, ed., *London and its Vicinity Exhibited in 1851* (1851), quoted by Jack Simmons in 'The Power of the Railway' in H.J. Dyos and M. Wolff, eds., *The Victorian City* (1973), vol I, 297.
13 Thornbury, *op.cit.*, 276. For Dickens and the locations of *Our Mutual Friend*, published in 1864–65, see E. Beresford Chancellor, *The London of Charles Dickens*, (1924).
14 Walford, *op.cit.*, 370, who quotes from F. Williams' *History of the Midland Railway* (1876).
15 John Hollingshead, *Ragged London in 1861*, (1986), 72.
16 Walford, *op.cit.*, 340.
17 Judge quoted in Jack Simmons, *St Pancras Station* (1968), 25.
18 Quoted in Simmons, *op.cit.*, 62.
19 A drawing of 1871 of these shops and pubs is reproduced in the *Survey of London*, xxiv, Plate 85. A detailed account of all the buildings east of York Way and around Battle Bridge Basin – the chief concentration of warehouses and industrial buildings in the King's Cross area – is given in *Industrial Archaeology Walks in London No. 8, Battlebridge Basin King's Cross*, published by the Greater London Industrial Archaeology Society (GLIAS) in 1986.
20 Report by Mr Sinclair for the Deacons' Court of Regent Square Church, 1848, quoted in the *Survey of London* xxiv, 103; E. Beresford Chancellor, *The History of the Squares of London* (1907), 248.
21 Henry Roberts, *The Dwelling of the Labouring Classes* (1853), quoted in J.N. Tarn, *Working-class Housing in 19th-century Britain* (1971), 6., and illustrated in J.S. Curl, *The Life and Work of Henry Roberts* (1983).
22 Charles Booth, *Life and Labour of the People in London*, Third series, vol II, (1902), 170.
23 Ian Nairn, *Nairn's London* (1966), 107.
24 Quoted in Malcolm J. Holmes, *Somers Town, A Record of Change* (1985).
25 Old houses in Somers Town and their replacements are illustrated in the LCC's book *London Housing* (1937).
26 S.E. Rasmussen, *London: The Unique City* (1937), 403. First published in Danish in 1934.
27 Nairn, *op.cit.*, 106.
28 The photographs of this church in the National Monuments Record were taken by Sir John Summerson shortly before its

demolition in 1936. Peacock's ancillary buildings survive in Wicklow Street behind the still empty site. The measured drawing of 'Nell Gwynn's Cottage' in the NMR was made by David Peace and J.H. Gifford. The former writes that, 'I think the owner who did the facade and lived there was known as 'Lord Compo', certainly as 'Stucco Jack'… Then one day we went round to admire it all, in 1938, and it was a heap of rubble: pulled down for an ARP exercise.'

29 Bennett was describing Clerkenwell rather than King's Cross and saw little charm in either the King's Cross Road – 'a hell of noise and dust and dirt, with the County of London tramcars, and motor-lorries and heavy horse-drawn vans sweeping north and south in a vast clangour of iron thudding and grating on iron and granite, beneath the bedroom windows of a defenceless populace.' – or places like 'Riceyman' [Granville] Square – 'The Square had once been genteel; it ought to have been picturesque, but was not. It was merely decrepit, foul and slatternly. It had no attractiveness of any sort. Evolution had swirled round it, missed it, and left it…' (2 & 44).

30 Report on *The Cultural Heritage* by Julian Harrap Architects for the London Regeneration Consortium plc., 1989.

31 George R. Sims, 'London Street Corners' in George R. Sims, ed., *Living London* (1902), vol II, 88.

ACKNOWLEDGEMENTS

I am indebted to Robert Thorne's researches into the buildings of King's Cross and thanks are also due to Andrew Sanders for his help, to David G. Thomas for telling me of the origins of the Scala cinema and to Ruth Guilding for introducing me to the secret splendour of the Paget Memorial Hall.

CHAPTER TWO

The Regent's Canal

Alan Faulkner

Running through the heart of the King's Cross development site are the quiet, mysterious, waters of the Regent's Canal. Today these waters are disturbed only by the passing of the occasional pleasure boat, but in days past the canal was a vibrant artery of commerce bringing trade and life to the whole area.

The Regent's Canal had its origins in 1801, although there had been some earlier plans for a similar scheme which proved abortive. In that year the Grand Junction Canal opened its branch to Paddington, then on the outskirts of London. The Grand Junction was a major trunk waterway that was opened for through traffic at the end of 1800. Its line ran from the river Thames at Brentford in Middlesex to the Oxford Canal at Braunston in Northamptonshire.[1] From Braunston there were canal links to Birmingham and the West Midlands, to Nottingham and the East Midlands, to Manchester and the North West, and to other parts of the country. As early as 1795 the Grand Junction had been authorised to construct a branch from Southall in Middlesex to a terminus at Paddington,[2] from where there was excellent road access to the City of London. Construction work on the branch started at the end of 1796 and it was opened with great celebration on 10 July 1801.[3] The Grand Junction went on to develop extensive wharves at Paddington and a substantial trade soon built up.

Early in 1802 there was a proposal for a railway to run from the Grand Junction at Paddington to the London docks. This idea was soon superseded by a scheme to extend the canal in an arc round north London to link up with the West India Docks. John Rennie, who was one of the leading canal engineers at the time, made the survey but the moving spirit behind the plans was Thomas Homer. He was based at Paddington and operated a fleet of craft on the Grand Junction. Rennie's plan involved a barge canal with double locks. It became known as the London Canal. A subscription list of £400,000 was opened and this was soon filled. The Grand Junction was then approached about providing a water supply. It refused to help as it had none to spare and was already getting involved in the public supply of water in the Paddington area. This rebuff, and opposition from landowners along the proposed route of the canal, led to the scheme being shelved in 1803.

The plan was revived by Homer early in 1810. He was assisted by John Holland, a surveyor who had been employed by the Grand Junction. Holland's report was encouraging and a more detailed survey was undertaken by the engineer James Tate. The canal was to run from the Grand Junction at the Harrow Road bridge near Paddington to the Limehouse Cut, part of the river

24. The east entrance to Islington Tunnel, a watercolour by T.H. Shepherd.

25. The City Road Basin of the Regent's Canal.

26. The Imperial Gas Works, King's Cross, a view published in 1828.

Lea navigation, at Limehouse. The line was to take a more northerly course than the London Canal, so as to avoid the built-up area.

Whilst all this was happening it was learned that the Duke of Portland's lease of Marylebone Park was due to expire in March 1811. The freehold of the park belonged to the Crown and was managed by commissioners. With the development of land bordering on to the park, such as the Portman estate to the west and the Southampton estate to the east, the commissioners were considering their own plans for the future of the park once the lease expired. In October 1810 the commissioners' small permanent staff, which included two architects, John Nash and James Morgan, was entrusted with drawing up plans for the park.[4] The general intention was for it to become, in part, a residential area with a new barracks and a new church.

Homer now approached Nash about his proposed canal, and Nash immediately realised the scenic and transport advantages that would accrue if the canal was to pass through the park. Homer then arranged a survey for an amended route with the canal passing through the middle of the park. A revised estimate was produced by Tate showing that a figure of £300,000 would be needed. Traffic potential was assessed at 700,000 tons per annum and was expected to yield £35,000 in tolls. With running expenses of £12,500 the anticipated surplus of £22,500 should have produced 7.5% return on the expenditure.

The plans for the park did not have to be submitted until July 1811 but in the meantime Nash started enlisting support for his ideas. He approached Sir

Thomas Bernard, a banker and philanthropist, in March 1811 and Sir Thomas then became one of the main promoters behind the canal. Nash also enjoyed the patronage of the Prince of Wales, who became the Prince Regent in 1811. With this support it was his plans which were accepted by the commissioners.

On 31 May 1811 a meeting of those interested in the new canal was held at the Percy Street Coffee House. Both Nash and Homer were present, and Nash now took a leading role in the canal's affairs. A new survey was put in hand and several changes were made to the line. The main one was to abandon the proposed link with the Limehouse Cut in favour of an independent junction with the river Thames. The revised estimate was £280,000 and in July a £400,000 subscription list was opened. Later it was restricted to £260,000 and this sum was raised without difficulty.

On 7 August Nash made the important announcement that the Prince Regent had not only approved the plans for the canal but had agreed that it could be called 'The Regent's Canal'. Soon after a proposal was made for a branch to be made towards the Gray's Inn Lane to bring the canal nearer the City. The idea became known as the Aske Terrace branch and plans were finalised just in time to be included in the Parliamentary notices.

The introduction of the Bill for the Regent's Canal unleashed a storm of protest in Parliament. Many vested interests saw the plan as a major threat and quickly made their fears known. Opposition from some quarters had been expected. The Grand Junction was concerned to protect its water supplies and also feared for the rents from its Paddington estate in the face of more conveniently placed wharves becoming available on the new canal. Several landowners were worried about the effect of the canal on their property. Some would negotiate and were given safeguards, some accepted the promise of additional bridges to aid subsequent development plans, but one remained totally obdurate. This was Edward Berkley Portman, who controlled a large estate at the west of Marylebone Park and who refused to permit the canal to pass through his property under any circumstances. As a result the line of the canal had to be moved northwards to avoid his land.

A small sub-committee, which included Bernard and Nash, had been set up to shepherd the Bill through Parliament and by persistence the many obstacles were gradually overcome. As a result the Regent's Canal Bill received the Royal Assent in July 1812 after a long hard struggle.[5]

The new company held its first general meeting on 10 August 1812 with Bernard in the chair. A committee was elected and Nash's associate, James Morgan, appointed as engineer to the project. Soon after Thomas Homer was appointed to superintend the company's affairs. Morgan began staking out the line of the canal from Paddington and seeking contractors to undertake the work. By the end of August tenders had been received and that of Hugh McIntosh of Poplar was accepted. On 7 October there was a ceremonial start to the work when Bernard put in the first spade in Marylebone Park.[6]

On the first stretch of canal one of the major works was a tunnel at Maida Hill under the Edgware Road. It had been intended to put this out to tender but it was subsequently decided to undertake the work under Morgan's direct responsibility. This was due to anxieties in London at the time following the collapse of a tunnel at Highgate during the construction of what is now the Archway Road. Work at Maida Hill started in December 1812 and it proved more expensive than expected mainly owing to a spring of water and some quicksand encountered in the excavation. This delayed progress and caused several serious casualties among the workmen. It was overcome by bringing in much extra labour and by using large amounts of timber to shore up and stabilise the excavation. At the same time alterations at the eastern end of the tunnel, caused by the problems with the Portman estate, led to the length of the tunnel being increased to 272 yards. This realignment also meant that an extra small tunnel was needed on Henry Eyre's estate. This became known as Eyre's tunnel; it was 53 yards long.

By June 1814 excavation of the canal from the Grand Junction to the Hampstead Road was nearly finished. The tunnelling work at Maida Hill was completed in August. A substantial cutting was required through Marylebone Park as the line of the canal had had to be moved northwards, partly because of the Portman difficulties and partly owing to a change of heart by the commissioners, who had now decided that they did not wish the canal to pass through the centre of the park. In addition the commissioners had insisted on a short branch canal being constructed round the eastern side of the park to serve a new basin.[7] Another unforeseen cost was the payment of £4,000 to Thomas Lord to move his cricket ground so that the site could be used for the canal and avoid still more earthworks.

By the beginning of 1815 the canal was virtually complete to the Hampstead Road. This included the branch canal. Most of the bridges were finished and only minor works, such as gravelling the towpath, remained. At Paddington a stop lock was started in July 1815 and an agreement was reached for a temporary supply of water. It was hoped the canal would be opened to Hampstead Road on 4 December 1815 – the works were completed on time and some boats did pass through to carry out the work on the towpath. With major problems elsewhere, however, it was not until Monday, 12 August 1816, that the first two mile stretch of the canal from Paddington, together with the 1,200 yard long branch, was formally opened.[8] This just happened to be the birthday of the Prince Regent.

Once work on the Maida Hill tunnel was complete, Morgan made a start on the much bigger task of the Islington tunnel in September 1814. Originally this was to have been 880 yards long and, as at Maida Hill, was estimated at £30 per yard. This had now been revised upwards to £40 but it was hoped the experience gained at Maida Hill could help contain costs. The work was again undertaken by direct labour and at first good progress was made. By the beginning of August 1815 the company was facing an acute shortage of money and most of the work had to be stopped, although Morgan was allowed to maintain a small number of men to complete the final heading between the last two working shafts. By the end of September all work had come to a complete standstill.

Whilst shortage of money was the main reason for suspending the construction work, the company had a major problem over its water supplies. To try and overcome this the committee had inspected plans of a canal lift invented by Colonel William Congreve. It comprised two counterbalanced caissons supported in two chambers on a cushion of air. Each caisson carried a column of water, equal to the depth of the canal, on which boats could float. By pumping air from one to the other, the caissons could be made to rise and fall and thus transfer the boats from one level to another. The idea was very attractive to the company as virtually no water was used in the process.

In March 1814 a contract was awarded to Henry Maudslay & Co of Lambeth to construct a trial lift at Hampstead Road. It was to have been completed by the end of March 1815 but Maudslays had endless difficulties in making the caissons watertight. Trials finally started at the end of March 1816. They showed that the machinery worked, but it took much longer, and much more power, to move the caissons than had been promised. Eventually the company decided to adopt conventional locks for the canal instead. (The Hampstead Road machinery was dismantled and sold off for scrap in 1819.)

The company now had to decide on its water supplies. Investigations revealed that there was insufficient water to justify the cost of a proposed feeder from Finchley where land had been purchased from a reservoir. Instead, the decision was taken to construct a pumping station on the banks of the Thames

at Chelsea, and to provide a pipeline to convey the water to Paddington. In the event, once the Chelsea works had been completed, they were transferred to the Grand Junction Waterworks Company in 1826 in exchange for that company's right to draw water from the Grand Junction Canal at Paddington.

All this did nothing to solve the underlying problem of money. With the greatly increased costs, the original capital was totally inadequate. In October 1816 an important meeting took place with the Chancellor of the Exchequer about the possibility of a government loan and eventually a £200,000 facility was approved in July 1817, with the company raising more share capital. With these funds work resumed on the Islington tunnel on 12 August 1817[9] – it was completed in September 1818 and was 960 yards long.

Although Hugh McIntosh had been awarded the contract to excavate the canal from Hampstead Road eastwards to Islington in January 1813, he had been unable to execute the work. This was due to a bizarre dispute involving William Agar who lived in Elm Grove, St Pancras, and owned land needed for the canal. Armed with its Parliamentary powers the company had given notice to Agar in April 1813 that it would set out the line of the canal through his ground. This produced a vigorous protest about trespass from Agar who obtained an injunction against the company from carrying the canal through his estate. This dispute rumbled on until March 1815 when the company, having tendered the purchase money, instructed McIntosh to enter the land and begin excavation. This resulted in the arrest of the company's overseer and foreman and more court proceedings. In the meantime, work was suspended.

Matters were no further forward in May 1818. An attempt to reroute the canal to avoid Agar's land proved abortive and it was becoming crucial to settle

27. The gasholders as seen from the goods yard. The frames with classical capitals were built in the 1880s, above gas tanks completed twenty years earlier. The holders with lattice frames are more recent.

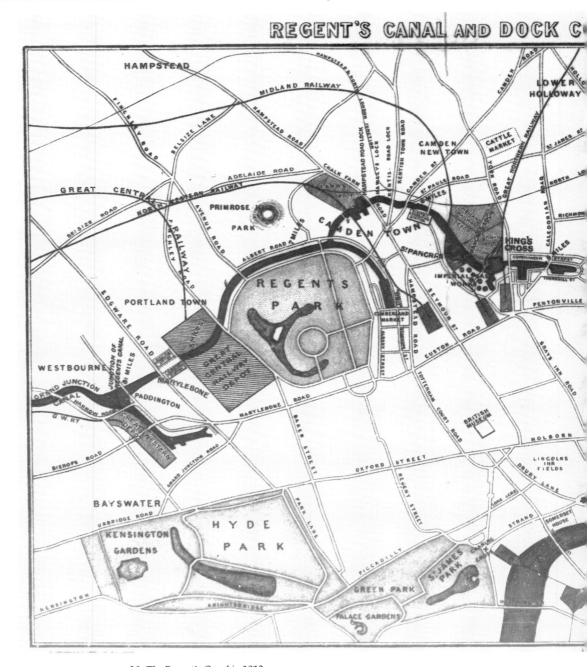

28. *The Regent's Canal in 1912.*

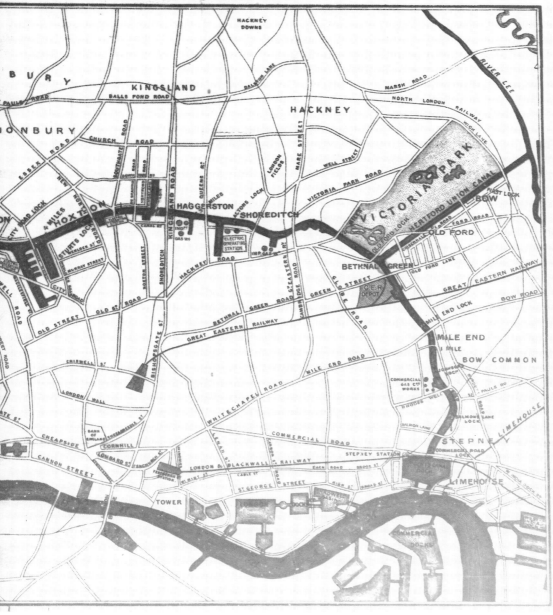

the matter. Sir Thomas Bernard made a personal approach to Agar and eventually it was agreed to pay the very high price of £15,750 for the five acres required. McIntosh made a fresh start on the work at the end of July. In the following month Richardson & Want contracted to build the bridges carrying Maiden Lane and the Caledonian Road. Then, in November, they started on the three bridges on Agar's estate and, in January 1819, on the construction of St Pancras lock.

McIntosh completed the bulk of the excavation work through the King's Cross area by December 1818 and the bridges were finished early in 1819. By June the lock was nearly complete but a decision to construct a second chamber alongside caused more problems with Agar. He contested the right to carry out the work. In April 1820 the company tried to force the issue, but Agar then insisted that the duplicate lock was dammed off (and it was not used until March 1825). The contract to build the lock house at St Pancras went to Francis Read in June 1820 on a tender of £102.

This was not the end of problems with Agar. He continued to complain and institute court proceedings for alleged grievances. It was not until 1832 that matters were finally settled, after nearly twenty years of constant litigation.

Meanwhile the other works were making good progress. In January 1818 George Roe's tender to excavate the canal from the Mile End Road to the Commercial Road was accepted. In May he was awarded the contract from Cambridge Heath to Mile End and in December he and his son John started on the stretch from Southgate Road in Hackney to Cambridge Heath. The contract for the final stretch of canal – from the east of Islington tunnel to Southgate Road – was let to McIntosh in September 1819. At the same time other contractors were brought in to construct the locks and bridges. By November 1819 all the main contracts had, at last, been let and were being executed.

There had been two major changes of plan. At Limehouse, where the canal joined the river Thames, it had been intended to have a small barge basin of about two acres in extent, separated from the river by a tidal lock. Following pressure from shipowners the company eventually agreed to enlarge the lock and the basin to accommodate shipping. At the same time the plans for the Aske Terrace branch were amended owing to the excessive price demanded for the land required. Instead, a branch to a basin on the north side of the City Road was substituted. Both alterations required the approval of Parliament.[10]

Hugh McIntosh had been awarded the contract for the original barge basin at Limehouse in March 1818, to include a lock large enough to accommodate ships. The work took much longer than envisaged due to the vast amount of excavated material that had to be taken away by barge, and the narrow link with the Thames restricted the speed of the operation. McIntosh was also awarded the contract for the City Road Basin.

With all this activity the company's funds were again becoming exhausted. Additional funds had been raised in 1819 to pay for the extra work at Limehouse, but this was not nearly enough. In the autumn of 1819 a request for a further government loan was turned down with the company being forcibly reminded that it had been a condition of the original loan that the canal was to be completed. As a result the shareholders had to agree to subscribe for more shares.

With these funds the works were finally completed and the canal was opened throughout for traffic on 1 August 1820.[11] The committee and their invited guests aboard a number of barges processed through Islington tunnel to the City Road Basin, and then on down the canal to Limehouse. This was followed by a celebration dinner at the City of London Tavern.

The canal was 8 miles 1,120 yards long. In this distance there were 12 twin locks, 36 bridges, three tunnels, an aqueduct and numerous culverts. In addition, there was the 1,210 yard long branch to Regent's Park basin, the 550 yard long branch to City Road Basin, the extensive Limehouse ship basin and the ship lock linking with the Thames. The work had cost more than three times the original estimate, which reflected the vastly inflated prices that had to be paid for the land, the greatly increased construction costs, particularly through Marylebone, and the extra facilities not envisaged in the original plans. Despite its cost the Regent's Canal was a major achievement.

Traffic quickly built up. In 1820 only 33,720 tons were carried, producing a mere £1,580 in tolls. But by 1825 tonnage had risen to 504,755 and receipts to £27,493. The principal commodities handled were coal and coke, sand, road materials, bricks, iron and nails, breeze, timber, lime, stone, chalk and general goods.

Traffic was also developing in the Limehouse basin. The first ship, *Little Mary*, had entered the basin on 17 August 1820, laden with coal.[12] By the end of 1820 15 loaded ships and 16 unloaded vessels had called. In 1830 these figures had risen to 592 loaded and 41 unloaded vessels.[13] A dockmaster was appointed to oversee the basin and he had a team of labourers who operated the lock, watchmen who controlled the craft entering and leaving, and a police officer.

The increased traffic caused problems at Islington Tunnel due to the length of time that barges took to pass through, and signalmen had to be employed to control entry and avoid collisions. In September 1824 trials began with a steam towing boat which hauled itself through the tunnel on a chain. These were sufficiently encouraging to fit up a craft permanently and delays were largely cured by this device.

Meanwhile traders were establishing wharves along the new canal. In many cases the creation of these involved excavating an indentation into the canal bank so that barges being loaded or unloaded would not impede traffic. At City Road Basin several carriers had reserved space even before the canal opened. They included Pickfords, the leading inland waterway carriers of the time, who shifted their main wharves from Paddington. Most of the other carriers followed them.

At the same time new industries were being attracted to the canal. In May 1822 the newly-formed Imperial Gas Light & Coke Company, which planned two new gasworks at Shoreditch, approached the company for permission to make a loading basin. This was opened in March 1823 and a substantial trade in coal imported through Limehouse basin developed. Soon after the gas company began a new works at Battle Bridge, near St Pancras, again beside the canal, where a short branch canal was opened in August 1824, and in the following year a large wharf was developed by the company to handle the growing trade.

In July 1824 the Independent Gas Light Company applied to make a short branch to its proposed new works at Haggerston. This was opened in October. Other gas companies used the canal. The Gas Light & Coke Company, with works at Curtain Road, Moorfields, and Brick Lane, Old Street, was supplied with coal from wharves on the canal from 1826.[14]

This all brought extra trade, but it also brought problems. In September 1828, after a tip-off, the company discovered that the Imperial Gas Company had been surreptitiously extracting water in large quantities at both St Pancras and Shoreditch through pipes laid in the canal below water level. No less than 265 tons of water daily had been taken by the Shoreditch works for the last four and a half years and 950 tons daily at St Pancras over nearly three and a half years. The gas company was clearly guilty but refused to pay the canal company's compensation claim of £2,841, which was based on a figure of one halfpenny per ton. Eventually, in 1829, a settlement of £1,700 was reached.

Apart from the gasworks there were several other basins developed at this time. Part of the material excavated from Islington tunnel had been used to build up ground at Battle Bridge so as to create a new basin there. Originally known as Horsfall's basin, after the landowner William Horsfall, it was opened at the same time as the main canal. Then, in 1825, a large new basin running to the east and parallel to the City Road basin was started by John Edwards. Opened in August 1826, it became known as the Wenlock Basin.

An important purchase was made in 1855. This was the Hertford Union Canal which linked the Regent's Canal at Old Ford to the river Lea navigation.[15] It was 1¼ miles long with a stop lock at the junction, and three locks near the Lea.[16]

Despite the additional share capital raised in 1819 the company was still faced with outstanding bills when the canal opened. In June 1821 £65,000 was needed to meet commitments, which included repayments on the government loan. A new approach was now made to the commissioners, who acted for the government, but there were legal restrictions in the Act which prevented them from assisting.[17] As a result the company promoted an Act to remove these restrictions and also to permit the raising of more capital. Once this was sanctioned the commissioners agreed to provide a further loan. At the same time further repayments were deferred for five years.

As trade built up the company soon began to find the constraints of the government loan increasingly difficult. All major decisions had to be referred to the commissioners for approval and the interest on the loan was a major drain on resources. In 1822 the company was instrumental in promoting a further Act which reduced the interest rate. In September 1826 the five year moratorium on capital repayments expired and this meant that the company had to find £11,750 each year to repay the loan over the proposed twenty-year term. As it was already having difficulties in meeting the interest, such an increase was insupportable. A new approach was made to the government which now offered a £25,000 abatement owing to the alteration dictated to the

29. Getting ready to 'leg it' through Maida Vale Tunnel in c1902.

line of the canal through Marylebone Park and the requirement to build the branch canal in the park. It was conditional on the loan being repaid. This was achieved by the issue of further shares and was completed in March 1828.

Freed from government control the company could now employ its revenues to providing a dividend to its long suffering shareholders. A maiden dividend of 63p% was declared in June 1829 and was paid in July: not a fortune, but a start. The tonnage in 1829 was 485,148 and receipts £23,357. Five years later the figures had increased to 610,089 tons and £28,678.

In this improving state the company now had to face a challenge from elsewhere. The first railway proposals that could have affected the canal came in the early 1820s with schemes to link up with the London docks. Little happened then but in the 1830s several lines were built which had a major impact on the canal.

The first was the London & Birmingham Railway which opened in July 1837. The canal posed a problem to the railway engineers for the company insisted on proper headroom for the new bridge at Camden. This meant a very steep drop down to the railway's terminus at Euston.[18] Soon after its opening the railway constructed a large warehouse on the north bank of the canal together with a short branch of canal that ran right into the building, enabling tranship-ment between railway waggons and canal barges to take place under cover. This facility set a pattern for several other companies which saw the canal as a means of supplementing their own services. The carriers Pickfords, who were now working to become railway agents instead of canal carriers, opened a similar transhipment depot at Camden in December 1841.[19]

The next railway to cross the canal was the Eastern Counties Railway at Mile End in June 1839.[20] An extensive goods depot and some coal drops were established at the Devonshire Street crossing point. At Limehouse, the London & Blackwall Railway, which crossed the canal immediately to the north of the basin, was opened in July 1840.[21] As part of the work the canal basin was extended northwards under the new railway viaduct and mainly at the railway company's expense. The railway closed in 1966 but the viaduct is now used by the Docklands Light Railway which opened at the end of August 1987.

The promoters of the Great Northern Railway decided that rather than bridge the canal on the approach to their King's Cross terminus they would tunnel underneath at Maiden Lane. The line was opened to a temporary terminus north of the canal in August 1850 and the contractor started on the construction of the aqueduct in April 1851.[22] The work was finished in March 1852 with the railway being extended through to King's Cross in October 1852. A second tunnel was opened in February 1878[23] and a third in June 1892.[24] In the Second World War stop gates were installed on the canal on either side of the tunnel to guard against flooding in the event of a breach following enemy bombing. The Great Northern also had a transhipment basin adjacent to the depot, known as the Granary, opened in 1852. There was another tranship-ment depot served by a short branch canal immediately below St Pancras lock. Coal drops were also built later at Camley Street on the west side of the canal, reached by a siding across the canal.

The Midland Railway both tunnelled under, and bridged, the canal at St Pancras. A siding was opened across the canal in January 1865, serving a large canalside warehouse built to store ale from Burton on Trent.[25] The warehouse had transhipment facilities with the canal. Then the Midland's line to link up with the sub-surface Metropolitan Railway tunnelled under the canal at St Pancras. It opened in July 1868. At the same time a bridge was built across the canal taking the railway into the St Pancras terminus. This opened for goods in September 1867 and for passengers in October 1868. The station was built up on masonry arches to avoid a steep drop down from the canal to street level. Work on a transhipment basin and coal drop on the canal by the crossing was started in January 1869; these were filled with water early in 1870. Leaks were then detected in the nearby St Pancras tunnel, but were soon cured, and the basin was opened in the autumn of 1870.[26]

The company did what it could to remain competitive. Beginning in 1832 the sides of the canal were reconstructed using perpendicular rag-stone walling, which prevented the banks being washed into the canal and increased the cross section of the waterway considerably. The main improvements, however, were to Limehouse basin. After its enlargement by the London & Blackwall Railway the company decided to construct an additional barge entrance lock to the east of the original entrance, so as to speed up the traffic and increase the number of vessels that could be handled. It was opened in 1849.[27] Then a large extension to the basin was made at the eastern side. This led to an agreement with the trustees of the river Lea for a link between the two navigations, as they were now only separated by a narrow strip of land. The work was put in hand in 1853 and was completed in that December.[28]

At the same time the company undertook a major extension to its Brent reservoir near Hendon. This reservoir had been constructed by the company under powers first obtained by the Grand Junction Canal Company.[29] Work had begun in 1834 and was completed in April 1835. It became known as the Welsh Harp reservoir and was a vital source of supply for the canal. The extension was completed in December 1853.[30]

In 1864 the agreement with the Lea trustees expired and the link at Limehouse was dammed off. By now the company was promoting another major extension to the basin involving a new and much larger ship lock and an increase in the water area to some eleven acres. An enabling Act[31] was obtained in 1865 and in August 1869 the new lock was opened.[32] This was the last extension. In 1873 part of the basin under the railway viaduct was filled in. The original ship lock was closed in 1897. Then the 1849 barge entrance was closed in 1924 leaving only the 1869 ship lock available for traffic. Latterly Limehouse basin has usually been known as the Regent's Canal Dock.

During all this time the challenge of the railways remained. The company was approached on several occasions with a view to its being purchased for conversion to a railway. The company also considered building its own railway

30. The Granary as depicted in the Illustrated London News *in 1853, showing the canal entrances into the building.*

along its banks, such as in 1845 when an unsuccessful approach was made to Parliament. In 1875 the Regent's Canal & Dock Company was incorporated to purchase the canal and to build a railway to link up with the Great Eastern Railway.[33] No action resulted and the Act was repealed in 1877.[34]

In 1882 the Regent's Canal City & Docks Railway Company was incorporated with powers to buy the canal and with ambitious plans to build a railway beside the canal from Paddington and into the City.[35] The canal was acquired for £1,170,585. Despite a series of further Acts simplifying the railway construction powers and extending the time for their completion,[36] the promoters were unable to raise the capital required. In 1892 the company was renamed the North Metropolitan Railway & Canal Company[37] and it was renamed again in 1900 to become the Regent's Canal & Dock Company.[38] By now all the railway powers had been surrendered or had lapsed.

Throughout this period traffic on the canal had been maintained at a high level. For instance, in 1888 tonnage was 1,009,451 on the canal and a further 663,508 in the dock. Receipts totalled £73,246, working expenses were £27,425 and a dividend of £2·625% was paid.[39]

For many years the main carriers on the canal were Pickfords. They gave up in 1847 and their place was taken by the Grand Junction Canal Company's Carrying Establishment. In 1876 the Grand Junction ceased carrying[40] and several new firms, based at the City Road Basin, were formed to take over its trade. By 1889 these had combined to form Fellows, Morton & Clayton Limited. It remained the leading long-distance canal carrier for the next 60 years.[41]

Towards the end of the 1890s tonnage on the canal started to drop. It had been 1,041,506 tons in 1898 but fell to 859,428 in 1918 and to 732,862 in 1927. The gasworks traffic, in particular, was hit. In 1861 the Gas Light & Coke Company's works at Curtain Road were provided with a railway siding. Then in March 1876 that company took over the Imperial Company with its works at St Pancras and Shoreditch, whilst in the same year it also took over the Independent Company with its works at Haggerston. In November 1870 a large new gasworks had been established at Beckton and gradually more and more gas production was concentrated there, enabling some of the older works to be closed.

In 1900 the Haggerston works were closed whilst in 1904 the St Pancras works ceased to manufacture gas.[42] Until then barges had continued to bring coal up from Regent's Canal Dock. They were discharged by a crane and grab operating from a gantry extending across the canal. At the time there were nine gasometers on the site – the oldest dating back to 1861, and these remained in use. Despite this, and in conjunction with coal factors and barge operators, Charrington Gardner & Locket,[43] modern equipment was installed in the Regent's Canal Dock in 1924 by the Gas Light Company. This facilitated the discharge of coal from colliers into barges to supply both the Shoreditch works and the works taken over in 1873 from the Western Gas Light Company at Kensal Green on the Grand Junction Canal's Paddington branch.

To counterbalance the loss of some of the gasworks traffic several electricity generating stations were established on the banks of the canal. Typical was the St John's Wood station, opened in 1904, and the nearby St Marylebone Borough station, opened in 1906. Both depended on the canal for their coal supplies. There were also stations at Shoreditch, City Road Basin and St Pancras. In 1929 190,374 tons were carried to power stations on the canal, earning the company £12,429 in revenue.[44] This fell sharply by the end of the 1930s, with only 11,925 tons being taken in 1938 earning a mere £993: this drop was due largely to the opening of the new Battersea power station beside the Thames in 1933. The St Pancras station ceased being supplied by canal in the 1930s, and was closed in March 1968.

The First World War brought major problems for the company, with acute staff shortages as men joined the armed forces or went to work in the munitions factories. The canal was brought under government control from 1 March 1917 with compensation then being paid for loss of profits. This control came to an end on 31 August 1920. Soon after the idea was mooted for a merger with the Grand Junction Canal Company. These plans went on to include three other companies which controlled the canal line up to Birmingham. Eventually, from 1 January 1929, the Regent's purchased the canal assets of the Grand Junction, and the entire assets of the other three companies, to create the present day Grand Union Canal.[45] From 1 January 1932 another three companies were acquired bringing the canal through Leicester and up to Langley Mill in Derbyshire under its control.[46]

The Grand Union went on to spend a considerable sum in modernising the canal between Braunston and Birmingham and widening the locks. It also invested heavily in a large fleet of canal narrow boats to develop traffic on its improved canal. Much new trade was generated including large tonnages of steel imported from the continent into Regent's Canal Dock. As part of this drive for traffic new shipping agents were appointed in 1932 to promote transhipment trade between ships and canal craft in the dock. Then in September 1937 a small steamer was purchased to establish regular services across to Antwerp. In November 1937 a new company – Grand Union (Shipping) Limited – was formed to develop this trade. It operated as the Regents Line. Later its services were extended to Rotterdam and other continental ports.

The Second World War brought further loss of traffic as again men were called up for war service and could not be replaced. Whilst the railways came under immediate government control the canals were not included until 1 July 1942. Compensation was then paid for loss of profits as tolls had been pegged but expenses had escalated with wartime inflation. Despite these difficulties a major dredging programme costing £30,000 was carried out in Regent's Canal Dock in 1944.[47] Wartime control came to an end on 31 December 1947, but on the following day the Grand Union, along with most of the country's railways and canals, was nationalised to become part of the British Transport Commission. The Regent's Canal and the dock was administered by the South Eastern Division of the Docks & Inland Waterways Executive, known as British Waterways.

On 1 January 1955 a new inland waterways board – British Transport Waterways – was established, following a recommendation by a committee headed by Lord Rusholme, a member of the British Transport Commission, which was set up in 1954 to consider the future of the inland waterways. From 1 January 1963 the British Transport Commission was abolished and the independent British Waterways Board was created. It is this body which controls the Regent's Canal today.

During all this time commercial traffic continued to decline as canalside works closed down or contracts were lost to competitors, most notably to road transport. Probably the last traffic was barges carrying dried milk from Limehouse to Glaxo's factory at Greenford, which operated up to 1973. A new development was the opening of a short canal on 1 April 1968.[48] It provided a link between the Regent's Canal Dock and the Limehouse Cut of the river Lea navigation – similar to the link severed in 1864. It enabled the former entrance to the Lea through Limehouse lock to be closed. Barge traffic through the dock to the Lea finished in November 1984.

In May 1969 Regent's Canal Dock was effectively closed to shipping. 388 ships had used the dock in 1967 but this number dropped dramatically in 1968. In practice a few boats continued to come into the dock to serve a scrap metal wharf until the early 1980s.

In the early 1950s the usage of the canal started to alter under the influence of the campaigning work of the Inland Waterways Association, founded in 1946. In 1951 a trip boat began operating from Paddington through Regent's Park to Hampstead Road as part of the Festival of Britain attractions. It was run by John James using the narrow boat *Jason* and was extremely successful. In May 1959 British Waterways inaugurated its water bus service to the London Zoo in Regent's Park – 75,000 passengers were carried in the first season. On 6 October 1958 the former Midland Railway transhipment basin was re-opened as the St Pancras Basin to provide moorings for 60 pleasure craft.[49] Other basins on the canal, such as the Wenlock, have subsequently been adapted to providing moorings for pleasure boats.

Further moorings were provided in September 1963 on the short stub of canal that remained of the branch in Regent's Park, which was last used by commercial traffic in 1930. The company commenced abandonment procedures in March 1937 and the Ministry of Transport issued an abandonment warrant in July 1940. Most of the branch was then filled in with rubble from bomb damage sites.[50] Part of the land was later incorporated back into the park and part was built over. Some small basins have also been filled in but the major ones have so far survived.

The increased use by pleasure craft led to pressure for the locks to be opened at weekends. In 1959 limited passage was permitted through the upper three locks to reach the St Pancras basin. In 1963 British Waterways agreed to the experimental opening of the Regent's and Hertford Union locks at weekends during August. Eventually the conversion of the duplicate lock chamber into a weir removed the danger of flooding in this heavily built up area. Once this

31. St Pancras Lock in 1912, overlooked by the western goods shed.

work was completed in 1976 the locks could be opened at all times without the necessity for supervision by lockkeepers.

In the mid 1960s the local authorities along the canal began to take an active interest in the future of the waterway, which had taken on a generally neglected appearance as trade had effectively turned its back on the canal. The Greater London Council and local amenity groups took the lead and soon highlighted its environmental potential. The first practical steps were initiated early in 1968 when the City of Westminster opened up the canal towpath from Lisson Grove to Regent's Park as a pedestrian walkway. In the spring of 1972 the London Borough of Camden extended the walkway to Hampstead Road. By then plans were well advanced for the path to be continued through Islington and ultimately down to Limehouse. Completed in 1982, it now forms the popular Canal Way.

Again spearheaded by the GLC considerable funds were invested in removing derelict buildings from the canalside and creating landscaped open spaces. A typical one was at Thornhill bridge near the Islington tunnel in 1979. Other developments have included the creation of the London Wildlife Trust's Camley Street Natural Park in 1983 on the site of the former Plimsoll coal drops, and the opening of British Waterways Canal Information Centre in the lock cottage at Hampstead Road in the summer of 1984. Elsewhere a major redevelopment, first announced in 1982, is now taking place in Regent's Canal Dock. Part of the basin is being filled in and a new and much smaller entrance lock was opened in May 1989.

More recently the proposals for the redevelopment of the railway lands at King's Cross are certain to lead to major changes on the canal, which forms the heart of the proposed park as shown on the Masterplan.[51] Indeed, the concept of the park is based on the comparable relationship of the canal to Regent's Park and other open spaces. Current plans include the re-creation both of the former basin in front of the Granary, and of the basin which was replaced in 1897–9 by the western goods shed. If, in the short term, the canal will be disrupted by the works authorised in the King's Cross Railway Bill, in the long term it is to be hoped that it will be more and more appreciated as the environmental and recreational asset that it is.

FOOTNOTES

1   For the full history see Alan H. Faulkner, *The Grand Junction Canal*, (1972).
2   35 Geo III c43 (28 April 1795).
3   *Northampton Mercury*, 18 July 1801.
4   Ann Saunders, *Regent's Park*, (1969).
5   52 Geo III c195 (13 July 1812).
6   Colonel John Drinkwater, *A Compendium of the Regent's Canal showing its connection with the Metropolis*, (1830).
7   The authorising Act was 53 Geo III c32 (15 April 1813).
8   Regent's Canal Company General Committee (Board) Minutes, 14 August 1816. Public Record Office RAIL 860/10.
9   Ibid, 6 August 1817 (RAIL 860/12).
10 59 Geo III c66 (14 June 1819).
11 *Morning Chronicle*, 2 August 1820, and several similar accounts in other newspapers.
12 Regent's Canal Committee minutes, 23 August 1820 (RAIL 860/18).
13 Select Committee on the Port of London, 1836 report.

14 Stirling Everard, *The History of the Gas Light and Coke Company*, (1949).
15 The canal was authorised by 5 Geo IV c47 (17 May 1824).
16 The purchase was authorised by 18 & 19 Vic c95 (26 June 1855).
17 1 & 2 Geo IV c43 (19 April 1821).
18 D.S. Barrie, *The Euston and Crewe Companion*, (1947).
19 Gerard L. Turnbull, *Traffic and Transport, An Economic History of Pickfords*, (1979).
20 H. V. Borley, *Chronology of London Railways*, Railway & Canal Historical Society, 1982.
21 Ibid.
22 John Wrottesley, *The Great Northern Railway*, (1979).
23 Ibid, 2, (1979).
24 Ibid, 3, (1981).
25 *The Times*, 3 January 1865.
26 E.G. Barnes, *The Rise of the Midland Railway, 1844–1874*, (1966).
27 Charles Hadfield, *The Canals of the East Midlands*, (1966).

28 Regent's Canal, half-yearly report to the shareholders meeting on 7 December 1853.

29 Under its original Act (33 Geo III c80, 30 April 1793) the company was authorised to make various reservoirs to supply the canal.

30 The extension was authorised by 14 & 15 Vic c32 (5 June 1851).

31 28 & 29 Vic c365 (5 July 1865).

32 Regent's Canal, half yearly report to the shareholders meeting on 27 October 1869.

33 38 & 39 Vic c206 (11 August 1875).

34 40 & 41 Vic c205 (6 August 1877).

35 45 & 46 Vic c262 (18 August 1882).

36 There were two in 1883, one in 1885, one in 1887 and one in 1890.

37 55 & 56 Vic c188 (27 June 1892).

38 63 & 64 Vic c118 (30 July 1900).

39 Royal Commission on Canals and Inland Waterways, *Report*, 1907.

40 This followed a massive explosion involving one of its boats in the Regent's Park. The *Illustrated London News*, 10 October 1874, carries an account of this famous disaster.

41 Alan H. Faulkner, *FMC, a Short History of Fellows, Morton and Clayton Ltd.*, (1975).

42 *The Gas Light and Coke Company*, op. cit.

43 The company was a major carrier on the canal. See Elspet Fraser-Stephen, *Charringtons, Two Centuries in the London Coal Trade*, (published privately 1952).

44 *The Times*, 30 March 1939 (covering the company's 1938 results).

45 18 & 19 Geo V c98 (3 August 1928), (Grand Junction Purchase Act). 18 & 19 Geo V c99 (3 August 1928), (Warwick Canals Purchase Act).

46 21 & 22 Geo V c107 (31 July 1931) (Leicester Navigation, Loughborough Navigation and Erewash Canal Purchase Act).

47 *The Times*, 9 May 1945 (covering the company's 1940 to 1944 results).

48 *Waterways, Staff Magazine of the British Waterways Board*, May-June 1968.

49 *Waterways, Staff Magazine of British Transport Waterways*, November 1958.

50 *The Star*, 24 July 1940.

51 See Chapter 7.

CHAPTER THREE

King's Cross and St Pancras: The Making of the Passenger Termini

Gordon Biddle

Any account of the railways entering London from the north or west must begin with the New Road, the broad highway now forming Euston and Marylebone Roads that continues on into Praed Street. It is lined by five termini, King's Cross, St Pancras, Euston, Marylebone and Paddington. How did the road come to form the barrier it seemingly is, and why do none of the railways go further into the centre of London, or indeed cross it?

The New Road was begun in 1757. By the 1830s high class development to the south by the Bedford, Portland and Portman estates, and the Crown, meant that any railway proposing to cross them would be faced by fierce, influential opposition and enormous expense. To the north, however, lay inferior property and, in some places, open land. By avoiding Regent's Park and Crown and Portman land on the north side, therefore, the railways could get as far as the New Road without prohibitive difficulty.[1] The first, the London & Birmingham, did so at Euston in 1837, after initially hesitating at Camden Town, followed in the next year by the Great Western at a temporary terminus just outside Paddington, which was not itself reached until 1854.

A further restriction on railway penetration was placed by the government in accepting the recommendations of the Royal Commission on Railway Termini in 1846. Its advice was against sanctioning railways within the districts lying between the New Road and the Thames, an area that has been called 'The London Quadrilateral'.[2] Instead, the Commission recommended a ring line connecting termini around the perimeter. The first part of the Circle Line, as it now is, was opened by the Metropolitan Railway between Paddington and Farringdon in 1863, running beneath the New Road as far as King's Cross. These two factors, particularly the second, ensured that only one railway ever crossed central London, and that tortuously, when in 1866 a connection was made from Farringdon to the London Chatham & Dover Railway at Ludgate Hill, and thence across Blackfriars Bridge to link up with railways south of the Thames.

As far as railways entering from the north were concerned, they had two obstacles to overcome as they approached London, the Regent's Canal and the Northern Heights. When Robert Stephenson built the London & Birmingham, an incline of 1 in 70–112 was necessary for the first mile out of Euston up to a distinct hump over the canal. At first it was operated by a stationary steam engine and rope. Beyond the canal, through Primrose Hill and Kensal Green

32. Main line train, headed by an A3 Pacific, approaching King's Cross from Gasworks Tunnel. Above the tunnel lies the goods yard, and in the distance are the towers of the Ebonite Works off York Way and the Caledonian Market.

tunnels, the line rose much less steeply or was level.

When Sir William Cubitt and his son Joseph came to plan the Great Northern Railway from King's Cross, the barrier of the canal was even more serious because it lay only some 200 yards from the planned outer ends of the platforms and about 30ft higher. The Cubitts' solution was to take the railway underneath it by dipping down slightly into Gas Works Tunnel and then rising through it and Copenhagen tunnel for over a mile at 1 in 107. It was an unfortunate decision that created a fearsome start for trains throughout the days of steam. After a brief respite through Holloway to Wood Green, the ascent through the Northern Heights began on a continuous gradient of 1 in 200 for eight miles to Potters Bar. Only with recent electrification has the difficulty fully been overcome.

The Great Northern received its authorisation to build a second railway route to the north, via the east coast, in 1846, breaking the monopoly of the London & North Western's west coast route from Euston. After some delay, land for the King's Cross terminus was acquired, mainly from the London Fever and Small Pox hospitals, for which new premises had to be provided. As a temporary measure, therefore, a terminus was opened on 7 August 1850 alongside the new goods station on the west side of Maiden Lane (now York Way), just north of the canal.[3] The passenger station had two simple, low shed roofs of slates with large louvres to let out smoke, and plentiful glazing, carried on wrought iron trusses and iron columns, of the kind already in extensive use elsewhere. They were side by side, covering three tracks, but, curiously, were staggered so that the entrance, ticket and other offices fitted into the recess formed at the inner end. Neither were they straight, but in plan delicately described a very gentle reverse curve.[4] The architect, Sir William Cubitt's nephew Lewis Cubitt, intended to use a similar construction at King's Cross, but when Maiden Lane showed signs of weakness a new design was needed quickly.[5]

Although roofs of this kind were cheap and could be erected rapidly, they had two great disadvantages: the trussed wrought iron spans imposed restrictions on width, and the rows of cast iron columns not only obstructed the platforms but, if a train jumped the rails and collided with one, easily snapped, bringing down others with it. There had already been several spectacular roof collapses from this cause, and no doubt Lewis Cubitt had in mind the failure of his cousin Joseph's roof at Bricklayers' Arms station in 1844. Consequently, engineers were experimenting with arched roofs which permitted broader spans and fewer rows of columns.

Richard Turner completed the first arched iron roof at Liverpool Lime Street in 1849. The widest shed at that time – of 60ft – was at Chester; Lime Street was 156ft 6in, a very notable advance. Five years later, a 211ft single-span roof was built at Birmingham New Street, bringing the railways into the age of great arched iron roofs, that lasted for fifty years. But at King's Cross, Lewis Cubitt chose timber, not iron. Possibly because time was short, he designed a double-span semi-circular arched roof with laminated timber ribs, following principles well established in bridge construction which had also been used at several smaller stations in the north of England, although nowhere on this scale. The spans were 105ft wide, composed of ribs 20ft apart springing from spandrel-shaped iron shoes attached to brick side walls, and a third wall running down the middle of the station pierced by broad elliptical arches. Some three-quarters of the roof was glazed and the remainder slated on boards. It was 72ft high and 800ft long.

There was a precedent at the Crystal Palace, where Sir Joseph Paxton had used laminated wooden arches to form the transepts. Sir William Cubitt had been chairman of the construction committee and was able to use his experience to execute Lewis's design quickly and economically. The laminations comprised sixteen 1½in boards screwed and bolted together and covered with

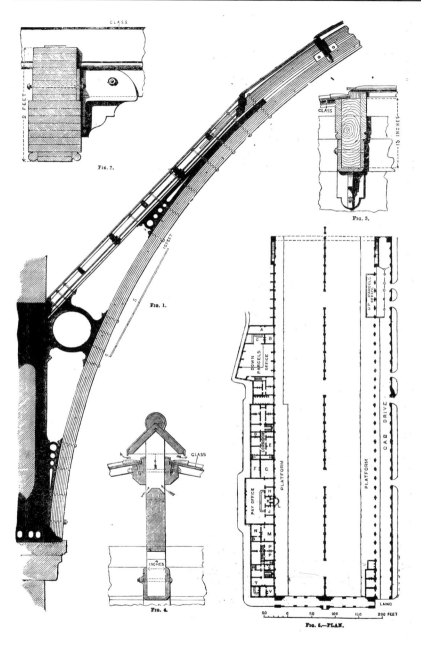

FIG. 2.

FIG. 3.

FIG. 1.

FIG. 4.

FIG. 5.—PLAN.

33. *Plan and roof detail of King's Cross showing the connection of the laminated ribs to the iron fixings in the walls.*

an iron band. As at the Crystal Palace, the ribs were fabricated on the ground using large chocks to obtain the correct radius before hoisting them into place.[6]

The thrust of the ribs on the west side of the station was taken by a three-storey office block, but on the east side heavy wooden flying buttresses were necessary over a cab drive. After twenty years they started to show signs of strain, which was only fully resolved when they were replaced by offices built over the cab drive. At the outer end of the roof, large gable screens with rectangular glazing filled the space above the springing, repeated at the opposite end in the form of lunettes in the great arched screen wall that formed the facade. Like the rest of the station, it is in yellow stock brick and can best be described in Lewis Cubitt's own words. 'The building will depend for its effect on the largeness of some of the features, its fitness for its purpose and its characteristic expression of that purpose.'[7] Today we would call it functional, which is what it was, inside and out. To a considerable degree the Great Northern was a 'no frills' railway; having paid out half a million pounds in parliamentary, legal and survey costs before turning a spadeful of earth, it was in no mind to engage in any sort of architectural extravagance. The twin train halls were devoid of any kind of decoration, other than elegant openings in the spandrels formed by the iron shoes corbelled out from the walls, and Cubitt's design relied entirely on the curves of the ribs to achieve a sense of airy lightness which, unencumbered by struts and ties and aided by the large areas of glass, it did admirably.

The frontage, too, relied on plainness for an effect that was provided more than anything by the outline of the roof profile in the two big semi-circular lunettes, a favourite device on the Continent and in the United States, but not repeated here. Directly below them the facade was enlivened by a pair of segmental-arched arcades giving on to the heads of the platforms. A charming little Italianate clock tower rising between the lunettes provided an element of decoration which relieved the otherwise austere design. The cab arch on the right was heavily rusticated, while the office block on the left, with its Venetian windows, added a note of assymmetry.

For the first ten years King's Cross had only two platforms, the western one alongside the offices for departures and the eastern one beside the cab drive for arrivals. The remaining space beneath the roof was occupied by carriage sidings, a not unusual feature at that time. For a while it was an efficient arrangement. Passengers passed through the lofty booking hall on the western side straight on to the departure platform, those arriving stepped out of the train to find cabs waiting alongside, and carriages could be stored and serviced, all under one roof. The station was opened on 14 October 1852, and at the time was the largest in Britain. Early in 1858 the Midland Railway also started running trains into King's Cross from Hitchin, to where it had built a new line from Leicester; previously its trains had entered London at Euston, over the London & North Western line from Rugby.[8]

When the first section of the Metropolitan Railway was opened, running beneath Euston Road to its own King's Cross station a little to the east, two underground connections were made from the Great Northern, which started running local trains through to Farringdon on 1 October 1863. Southbound, a single line tunnel curved down beneath York Way on the east side of the terminus; in the opposite direction a longer, sharply curved tunnel rose on a steep gradient to emerge on the west side. It passed under Lewis Cubitt's Great Northern Hotel, from which it got its name of the Hotel Curve, and throughout the steam era was a constant nightmare to enginemen struggling to keep their trains on the move in the smoke-filled darkness. The opening of the link to Ludgate Hill and south London in 1866 brought goods trains to the tunnels, making conditions worse. On at least one occasion, in 1937, greasy rails caused a locomotive to slip so badly on the climb that, unknown to the crew who thought they were still moving forward, the train started to slide backwards and collided with another one following behind.

In both directions, Farringdon trains at first had to reverse into or out of the main station. A platform for southbound trains called York Road was opened just outside the station on 1 January 1866, but was not followed by a corresponding one on the west side until 1 February 1878. This was located immediately where the Hotel Curve emerged from the tunnel and it was known

as King's Cross (Suburban).

Meanwhile, increasing traffic was outgrowing the capacity of the terminus. A second arrival platform was built in 1862, and in 1873 two platforms for local trains were built outside the main station on the west side, under a separate roof and in effect forming a separate station with its own entrance and booking office. Confusingly, it was called King's Cross (Local), and the King's Cross (Suburban) platform lay beyond. But in 1893 there was still only one main line departure platform, despite there being 40 trains a day using it. In that year two more platforms were added down the middle of the station, on either side of the central wall, and at the same time the iron footbridge with its well-known clock was built to link the offices on each side. A third platform was added to the 'Local' station two years later, together with a fourth beyond the Hotel Curve platform.

Towards the end of the 1860s the wooden ribs of the eastern trainshed roof were clearly deteriorating. This was thought to be caused by inadequate ventilation (although in view of the speed of construction, one wonders whether the wood had completely dried out) and in 1866–67 they were replaced by iron. A large travelling timber stage was used, as had been done to erect previous arched roofs, first at Birmingham New Street in 1854, and concurrently at St Pancras. Another was erected when the western trainshed ribs were renewed in 1886–87. It was built of large timber baulks braced together, carrying five working platforms at different levels and roughly fitting the profile of the roof. The main timbers were 1ft square and the braces 10in by 5in, supported at platform level by iron girders which were carried on a total of 52 wheels running on four rails, two on each side, so that the whole erection

35. A Builder engraving of 1861 recording the tunnelling works at the junction of the Metropolitan Railway with the feeder line from the Great Northern.

could be moved along the station as work progressed. The working platforms were strong enough to carry cranes. The contractors who built it were Sherwyn Reynolds and Son of Lincoln. They had worked for the Great Northern before, and were known for their work in bridge building.[9]

The main trouble with King's Cross was that the station was not long enough. There was simply insufficient distance between the buffer stops and Gas Works tunnel for the efficient movement of trains that were steadily getting longer, so that those waiting to depart often blocked the entry of trains trying to get in. Add to this the constant movement of locomotives in and out of the servicing yard on the west side, rigid adherence to separate arrival and departure sides with consequent criss-crossing of engines and trains immediately outside the station, compounded by trains entering the local station having to cross the main departure tracks, and it is hardly surprising that at busy periods delays were endemic. The advantages gained by first doubling the Gas Works tunnel in 1878, then tripling it in 1892, were of short duration; not until 1922–24 was a serious attempt made to alleviate the problems by altering the track layout, moving the engine yard further west – for the second time – and constructing a new island suburban platform. On the departure side another platform was built in 1926, bringing the total to 15, reduced to 14 in 1934 when a short platform was abolished to enable another to be lengthened. All this work was completed by the London & North Eastern Railway, of which the Great Northern now formed part, and no further improvements in layout occurred until the 1970s, concluding with electrification of suburban services in 1978. The electrification programme included diversion of inner suburban

36. *Hertford train leaving the Metropolitan line platform on the west side of King's Cross.*

trains to Moorgate from Finsbury Park. This allowed the closure of the Hotel Curve and York Road tunnels, York Road platform and five of the suburban platforms, leaving two platforms adequate for outer suburban electric trains, (in 1989, however, a third was reinstated). At the same time the entire track layout was simplified, enabling closure of one of the Gas Works tunnels. The introduction of InterCity 125 high speed trains virtually did away with separate locomotives at King's Cross, and at last the station was adequate for its traffic.

As the years went by, the station forecourt became increasingly despoiled. An iron and glass canopy successfully hid Lewis Cubitt's arcades, in front of which there grew a deplorable clutter of small buildings, huts and shelters. Inside the station, the narrow cross-platform behind the buffer stops that was sufficient to connect the two platforms in Cubitt's day was quite inadequate as a concourse when more platforms were added; indeed, King's Cross had no concourse, while confusion was increased by having the booking office part way down the western side. The 1970s alterations changed all that. The clutter was swept away and a covered concourse was built in front of Cubitt's arcade, containing full facilities, including a travel centre and access to the Underground. Reservations about the architectural styling were expressed in some quarters, and it was a pity that the arcades could not be exposed to view again – although it must be admitted that it would have been virtually impossible to have both a concourse and the arcades – but it certainly was a vast improvement on the old.

The Midland Railway stopped using King's Cross in 1868, to the relief, no doubt, of the Great Northern's operating managers for whom congestion had become chronic, if not to the commercial authorities who were far from relieved at the prospect of competition from the grand new terminus overshadowing them across the road. In 1862 the Midland board decided that the only way to avoid the delays to its trains on the overcrowded Great Northern line from Hitchin was to build an independent route of its own into London, with a terminus, like the others, on the New Road. The company's consulting engineer was William Henry Barlow. Although he had worked for the Midland since 1842 and was a leader in his profession, it was the London Extension and St Pancras which brought him fame.[10]

Barlow faced the same problems as Robert Stephenson and Sir William Cubitt: the descent from the Northern Heights and crossing the Regent's Canal. Little could be done about the former. A fairly steep rise out of London, with tunnelling, was unavoidable, but Barlow was determined not to repeat Cubitt's mistake at the canal. He also had two other major difficulties to resolve. The Midland wanted a junction with the Metropolitan in order to secure the same access to the City and south London as the Great Northern, while the station site lay over the River Fleet which served as a sewer for much of north London. These were purely engineering problems, but when it came to acquiring the land human and religious factors were present. Several thousand people lived in Agar Town and Somers Town, on the site required for the goods and passenger stations, which also included St Luke's church on Euston Road, and Old St Pancras churchyard and burial ground. The first two were the easier to deal with. The question of re-housing was ignored; the Midland quite ruthlessly evicted all 10,000 residents, earning some approbation so far as Agar Town was concerned, as it was a notorious slum and in sanitary terms its clearance was an improvement, though Somers Town, where 4,000 dwellings were demolished, was modestly respectable. St Luke's was rebuilt at the company's expense, as required under the Act granting powers to build the station. It was the burial ground that gave the most trouble.

Barlow's plan was masterly. He resolved the difficulty posed by the canal by deciding to build the station above ground level, with a ramp up from the street, thereby allowing him to bridge the canal without creating a dangerously steep descent into the terminus. The steepest part, in fact, is 1 in 106 for a short distance. It was an idea that had been successfully tried on a much smaller scale at Leeds Central station when it was rebuilt in 1857, immediately outside which a river and a canal had to be crossed; a solution which Barlow undoubtedly would have been aware of, although that is not to say it directly inspired his thinking.

Additional benefits were twofold. First, the space beneath the station at street level could be used for warehousing Burton beer, a traffic that was highly lucrative to the Midland, with a hydraulic lift to take wagons up and down. To create the greatest economy of space, Barlow dispensed with the customary brick arches and piers to form a deck above, in favour of 13ft 6in high cast iron columns and wrought iron girders in a grid pattern supporting iron plates to carry the platforms and tracks. They were strong enough to take the weight of a locomotive at any point, and the spacing of the columns was the same as in Burton beer warehouses. To use Barlow's words, 'in point of fact, the length of a beer barrel became the unit of measure, upon which all the arrangements of this floor were based.'[11] Having thus decided, Barlow proceeded to design a roof that required no intermediate supports that otherwise would take up valuable platform space and, in passing through to the cellar, could upset his storage pattern.

The second benefit of an elevated station, Barlow perceived, was that the passenger deck formed a ready-made tie for a single-span arched roof. It was a daring concept that had not been attempted before, giving a clear, unobstructed space of 245ft 6in across the station, the widest single-span trainshed roof yet attempted: indeed it has since been exceeded only by three others, all in the United States and none of them as high, rising as it does 105ft from the rails. This gigantic trainshed was 689ft long, and the crown of the arch was slightly pointed to give lateral wind resistance and, simultaneously, a slightly Gothic outline that matched the detail of the side walls and, eventually, the hotel that was built on the front.

The River Fleet was put into an iron conduit at the insistence of the Metropolitan Board of Works, which laid down exacting conditions regarding its construction to ensure that nothing would interrupt the flow. Here again, the single-span roof meant that no special reinforcement of the conduit was required at points where columns might have been erected over it. But dealing with such problems was straightforward compared with crossing the burial ground. Barlow could either go over it on a bridge or avoid it entirely by demolishing the adjacent gas works. Naturally he chose the former. The burial ground also lay in the path of the branch to the Metropolitan, which was planned to leave the main line south of Kentish Town at what is now St Paul's Road Junction, and descend at 1 in 75 through a double-line tunnel underneath the burial ground and the canal, thence curving beneath St Pancras station to join the Metropolitan by a second underground junction in front of King's Cross. In the event, Parliament insisted on a second pair of tracks being laid alongside the Metropolitan to take Great Northern and Midland trains to Farringdon, necessitating the alteration of the Great Northern junction. Known as the City Widened Lines, they were completed in 1868 and gave both companies access to Ludgate Hill and south London without obstructing the Metropolitan's Circle Line.

The St Pancras branch tunnel was constructed by the cut-and-cover method, causing a public outcry when it was realised just how the burial ground was being disturbed. The graveyard served a large part of north London, and over several centuries a number of well known people had been buried there. It was also desperately overcrowded. Despite strict conditions that the main line bridge should have no more than two or three girder spans and that the tunnel roof should be at least 12ft from the surface, disruption of graves was inevit-

37. The basement level columns for St Pancras being erected in 1865, with the newly-completed Stanley Buildings in the background.

able. The Midland was required to re-inter remains at its own expense, but the conditions imposed were not adequate to allay serious public disquiet, if indeed they could be at such a place. Horrific and macabre tales of desecrated graves were rife, men were reluctant to work for long in the foetid ground, and when it was opened up there were fears of an epidemic. Work was stopped while an enquiry was held, after which it was done more carefully, but by the time the tunnel was finished the Midland had lost much of the credit it had gained for destroying the Agar Town slums.

Meanwhile, work was progressing on the station, and in the first part of 1867 229 men and 111 horses were at work, aided by four locomotives and 18 other steam engines. The station floor was supported by 720 columns, each capable of carrying 55 tons, and once the cellars were well under way the side walls could be commenced, interspersed with brick piers carrying heavy iron anchor plates. From them sprang the 25 main ribs, 6ft deep in latticed iron, spaced at 29ft 4in centres, each weighing nearly 55 tons. Between them were three 10½in deep intermediate ribs. The contract for the roof was placed with the Butterley Company of Derbyshire, whose name is carried on iron plates along both sides of the station.

The roof was erected by using a huge mobile scaffold, later augmented by a second one, weighing about 1,300 tons and providing an effective test of the station floor. Constructed from large timbers to fit the arch of the roof, each scaffold was in three sections, 40ft deep, which could be moved independently. They ran on rails, and to move a section a man with a crowbar was stationed at each wheel which, to the foreman's beats of a hammer on an improvised gong, was slowly levered along at about 1½in a time.[12]

Barlow was assisted in the detailed design by R.M. Ordish, an expert on iron structures who had worked on Birmingham New Street, the Crystal Palace and the dome of the Albert Hall, and went on to design the station roofs at Amsterdam Central and Glasgow St Enoch. A deep gable screen was provided

38. The huddle of buildings on the curve at the southern end of Pancras Road, depicted by C.J. Richardson in 1871 just before they were demolished.

at each end, at the inner end joined to the hotel. A hoist was built at the outer end of the station to lower waggons into the warehouse below, where they were moved about on a criss-cross of rails and turntables by hydraulic cap-stans. Beyond the station a brick water tower was built in matching style. The tunnel to the Metropolitan was finished first, opening on 13 July 1868, followed by the station itself on 1 October, without any kind of ceremony; in fact, the first train entered at 4.15 in the morning.

There was, of course, as yet no proper frontage to Euston Road, merely the vehicle ramp, a temporary booking office and other necessary rooms, and the foundations of the massive hotel that is dealt with in Chapter Four. The architect, George Gilbert Scott, designed station offices and refreshment rooms to occupy part of the ground floor and a separate booking hall on the west side of the station concourse that was finished in 1869. It was quite the most elaborate part of the station, as distinct from the hotel, with a high, open-trussed roof on carved hammer-beams, six tall pointed windows, and a grand ticket office in linen-fold panelled oak that was matched by a dado around the main hall. Along one wall, blind arcading contained four intriguing figures of railwaymen carved on the stone corbels: an engine driver, guard, pointsman and what appears to be a signal boy. Scott designed ornate gasoliers made by Skidmores of Coventry, who did much of the ornamental ironwork in the hotel. During Second World War air raids the booking hall roof was destroyed

39. Cross-section through St Pancras station and the Midland Grand Hotel, from the Engineer *for 1867.*

and it was rebuilt as a flat structure with an ill-at-ease transluscent ceiling. Fortunately, this was replaced in 1983 by a panelled ceiling that matches the restored interior. At the same time, the ticket office was moved to the opposite side of the hall.

Although its dimensions were not exceeded in Europe, Barlow's roof started a fashion in trainsheds. Curiously, it was repeated at three northern termini into which Midland trains ran from London. A number of writers have re-marked that passengers departing beneath the great roof at St Pancras arrived at Manchester Central, Liverpool Central or Glasgow St Enoch beneath a similar one; smaller, and not identical, but bearing a striking affinity to the one they had left a few hours before.

Apart from immediate contrasts in size and scale, the most important histor-ical difference between King's Cross and St Pancras is that the latter has not needed enlargement. Thanks to the foresight and skill of Barlow and the Midland Railway, the station has been adequate for the demands of over a century of operation. Initially there were five platform faces and eleven tracks, of which six were carriage sidings. In 1892, two more platforms were added in place of sidings, since when there has been no further change apart from the disuse of the short platform 1 in recent years, although it could easily be brought back into use if need be. Major re-signalling has been carried out twice, in 1957 and 1982, accompanied by re-arrangement of the approach lines. The earlier scheme included the abolition of a little-known signal box deep under the station in the tunnel. It was placed there in 1889 to increase the tunnel's capacity by making two block signalling sections, and was approached by a spiral staircase. The box was a lonely, eerie place, the signalman's turn of duty broken only by the intermittent ringing of bell codes from the boxes on either side and the roar of passing trains, unseen except, perhaps, for a momentary

40. The full grandeur of Barlow's St Pancras trainshed photographed in 1866 just before the station opened. The slight point to the arch was introduced, Barlow said, partly for 'architectural effect'.

glare from the engine's firebox and dim lights from the carriages through smoke that seeped in through the windows. It closed early in 1958, and the tunnel is now used by electrified Thameslink services.

In 1983 St Pancras underwent the same process of overhead electrification as King's Cross five years earlier. Both stations were fully wired, at King's Cross in a fashion that could hardly have been more detrimental to its internal aspect. The overhead catenary is suspended from ugly steel gantries ranged down the platforms, stark and uncompromising, completely ruining the vista. Fortunately British Rail profited from this mistake and carried out the same job at St Pancras in exemplary manner. The greatest care was taken, with the result that the catenary is suspended directly from the roof in so unobtrusive a manner that one is hardly aware that it is there. The drama of Barlow's great span is unimpaired.

41. St Pancras booking hall, with its booking office windows like travellers' confessionals.

42. St Pancras by night, from the roof of Stanley Buildings.

From the beginning St Pancras has aroused controversy, as Jack Simmons has pointed out. It started with the evictions and has gone on intermittently ever since. A leading article in *The Engineer* in 1867, when the station was under construction, commenting on the need to balance the advantages of having no columns against the high cost of a single-span roof, considered that the Midland had gone too far.'There is no possible utility in constructing a roof of dimensions similar to those of the future St Pancras station.'[13] A year later, the completed work was criticised for its 'gigantic rotundity', in which 'height appears to be the object aimed at.'[14] As a technical journal it should have known better; clearly the comment was aimed at the Midland's desire, as a provincially-based railway, to proclaim its presence in London as prominently as it could afford. The same theme was repeated when the new Marylebone station was reviewed in 1901. St Pancras was called 'unsightly' and the view taken that large single span roofs in general 'partake more of the nature of a *tour de force* than of a plain and sensible recognition of the absolute requirements of the undertaking.'[15]

King's Cross, on the other hand, although much less efficient as a working railway station, has generally received the greater approval in architectural circles, apart from criticism of the clock turret which is still sometimes voiced. An architectural writer in 1914 called the King's Cross facade 'Dignity and Impudence,' after Landseer's painting: 'two Cyclopean arches' and between them an architectural climax which failed – 'drama turned into farce.'[16] Yet just before the Second World War Professor (later Sir) Albert Richardson consi-

PARCELS
DELIVERY OFFICE

43. Renewal of the eastern trainshed roof at King's Cross in 1868. The shape and fixings of the new wrought iron ribs were the same as their timber predecessors.

dered King's Cross 'the finest railway station in London,' satisfactory in scale, built in honest stock brick with the hotel 'decently out of the way' and the front screen 'a model for all students of elementary building construction.'[17] The sideswipe at St Pancras, particularly Scott's hotel, was obvious; the fact that the King's Cross layout was a mess and the station hopelessly inadequate was ignored.

The truth is that each station has its own quality, one balancing the other: King's Cross, the pioneer with its two modestly-dimensioned barrel roofs, designed for economy and speed of construction, side-by-side with St Pancras, the ultimate single-span, widest in Europe, highest in the world, the proud symbol not merely of the Midland Railway's grand ambition but of the whole railway age. We now appreciate them for what they are, opposites. Of the Great Northern terminus, the late Henry-Russell Hitchcock said: 'King's Cross has a vigour and a boldness of scale in parts, as well as an absence of frivolous detail...It is surely the Early Victorian climax of station shed development,[18] while of St Pancras John Julius Norwich has written: 'In all England there is no more triumphant affirmation of the power, vitality, self-confidence and sheer panache of the Victorian age.'[19]

Rightly, both stations are listed Grade I, no longer rivals but now sharing a controversy that involves them equally; a link to physically join them. It may be that they are so disparate that they should not be joined at all. Many think so. Whatever the outcome it will test the designer's skill to the utmost and no doubt carry the controversy on into the twenty-first century.

FOOTNOTES

1   For a comprehensive analysis see J.R. Kellett, *The Impact of Railways on Victorian Cities*, (1969), chapter IX.

2   J. Simmons, *The Railway in England & Wales, 1830–1914. Vol 1, The System and its Working*, (1978), 116 et seq.

3   A.A. Jackson, 'The Location of the London (Maiden Lane) Temporary Terminus (GNR)'. *Journal of Railway and Canal Historical Society*, XXIX, no 142 (July 1989), based on research by Malcolm Tucker.

4   The original drawings are in the library of the Institution of Civil Engineers.

5   J. Wrottesley, *The Great Northern Railway, Vol. 1. Origins & Development*, (1979), 79.

6   *The Builder*, 22 Nov 1851, 731.

7   Quoted in C.H. Grinling, *The History of the Great Northern Railway*, (1903 edn), 114.

8   For a detailed account of King's Cross, see A.A. Jackson, *London's Termini*, (1985), chapter 4.

9   Drawing in the Lincolnshire County Record Office, SHER G/45.

10 For a detailed account of the history of St Pancras, see Jack Simmons, *St Pancras Station*, (1968).

11 Paper by Barlow, given at the Institution of Civil Engineers, quoted in Simmons, op. cit., 31.

12 Charles E. Lee, 'St Pancras Station', *Railway Magazine*, 114 (Sept 1968), 511–15.

13 *The Engineer*, 30 August 1867.

14 *The Engineer*, 4 September 1868.

15 *The Engineer*, 2 August 1901.

16 Paul Waterhouse, 'London Railway Stations', *RIBA Journal*, XXI (28 February 1914), 243.

17 'Railway Stations', *RIBA Journal*, XLVI (8 May 1939), 650.

18 Henry-Russell Hitchcock, *Early Victorian Architecture in Britain*, 1 (1954), 557.

19 John Julius Norwich, *The Architecture of Southern England*, (1985), 389.

CHAPTER FOUR

The Great Northern and Midland Grand Hotels

Oliver F. Carter

When the Great Northern Hotel welcomed its first visitors at Easter 1854, railway-owned hotels were already an established feature in several provincial towns and ports, including Birmingham, York, Stoke-on-Trent, Hull and Dover. In Ireland, new hotels at Galway and Killarney catered for the tourist.

Although the new hotels were built to provide accommodation for the travelling public in locations with little or no existing provision, the press deplored the demise of coaching inns. The *Illustrated London News* put the blame on the railway companies, 'for the impediments they have thrown in the way of a cheaper hotel system. At the extremity of every line, hotels have been erected in situations which virtually monopolise all the best traffic. These hotels, built on a scale of great magnificence, are burdened with a proportionate rent'.[1]

Parliament never held that the railways should be barred from keeping hotels, provided that their actions were confirmed. Twenty-four years after the Great Northern Hotel at King's Cross was built, the GNR (Further Powers) Act 1878 (41–42 Vic. cap cli) confirmed that, 'the company may hold, enjoy, maintain as part of its undertaking, the hotels now belonging to or held by them at King's Cross (London), Peterborough, Lincoln and Leeds'. The Midland Railway obtained similar powers a year earlier in the Midland Railway (New Works) Act (40–41 Vic. cap lii), which confirmed their ownership of hotels at Derby, Leeds and Morecambe, as well as the Midland Grand in London, by then opened for four years.

As the wording of these Acts confirm, the Great Northern Railway and the Midland Railway already had some earlier experience in hotel management before building at their respective sites at King's Cross and St Pancras. The GNR's hotel at Peterborough had been built in 1851, the hotel at Lincoln purchased in 1848 and that at Leeds built in 1869. One more hotel, at Bradford, was purchased in 1892 and the company enjoyed a reputation as a reliable hotelier. The Midland purchased its hotel in Derby in 1861, built that at Leeds in 1863 and took over the hotel at Morecambe in 1871; eventually, it owned ten hotels. Ultimately the Midland rose to a position of pre-eminence in the hotel industry, due largely to the energy and foresight of Sir William Towle (1849–1929), who entered service with the Midland at their Derby hotel in 1864.

The Great Northern Hotel at King's Cross and the Midland Grand Hotel at St Pancras had quite different pedigrees. The former was designed by an architect little known at the time, Lewis Cubitt (1799–1883), while the latter was the work of Sir George Gilbert Scott (1811–78), the most famous British architect then alive. Neither had designed an hotel before. Cubitt's solution drew from his earlier experience as a house designer. Scott's design drew from a mixture of his profound knowledge of Gothic architecture and an intention to provide his client with the best new building in London.

The Great Northern Hotel, now in its 135th year of service, owes its long life to its simple, and consequently more easily maintained, layout and construction. The Midland Grand closed after 62 years' service, following a decision by the LMS Railway's Hotel Committee not to modernise the accommodation.[2]

THE LONDON HOTELS

Of the London railway hotels the Great Northern and the Midland Grand were respectively the second and the seventh among the ten which opened.

Euston, the world's first railway-owned hotel, opened in 1839; it was followed by the Great Northern, and the Great Western Royal, Paddington, both in 1854; the Grosvenor at Victoria Station in 1861; the Charing Cross in 1865; the City Terminus at Cannon Street in 1866; the Midland Grand in 1873; the Holborn Viaduct in 1877; the Great Eastern, Liverpool Street in 1884 and the Craven, an existing hotel, leased in the 1890s.

The railways encountered little competition from other hoteliers until the 1880s. In fact, the only important new hotels to be built in London were the Westminster Palace, opened in 1859, the Palace, Buckingham Gate, in 1861, and the famous Langham Hotel, Portland Place, in 1865, which incorporated unprecedented heights of luxury. Then, in 1881, the Grand Hotel, on the site of old Northumberland House, was opened by Frederick Gordon (1835–1904). Gordon created the world's first great hotel empire, and his debut was followed by the First Avenue Hotel in 1883 and the Metropole in 1885. He later acquired from Jabez Balfour MP, the Victoria, in Northumberland Avenue, opening it in 1887. Balfour, the 'genius who jumped at Park Lane and landed at Broadmoor',[3] had formed the Liberator Building Co, and, having built the Hyde Park Hotel (originally a block of flats called Hyde Park Court), ran out of funds for the 800-roomed Hotel Cecil, which was opened in 1896 after he had been imprisoned for fraud.

A further landmark was reached in 1896 with the formation of the Ritz Hotel Syndicate and the opening of the luxurious Carlton in 1899. Frederick Gordon again made headlines in 1899 with the floating of Frederick Hotels (named after the Henry Frederick Syndicate) and the opening of its Hotel Great Central at Marylebone, and the Hotel Russell in Russell Square. This rapid growth of hotel chains induced a measure of competition which proved useful to railway companies wanting to lease out their hotels. The Grosvenor at Victoria, and the Lord Warden at Dover, were both leased out to Gordon Hotels.

The railways took no part in subsequent London hotel developments from the 1920s onwards. Nevertheless, it is interesting to reflect on the demise of the Gordon Hotels, and the resilience displayed by the railway hotels, well-run and with consistently good reputations. Of Gordon's empire, the Grand closed in 1927, the First Avenue in 1935, the Metropole in 1936 and the Northumberland Avenue (by then renamed the Victoria) in 1940. The Cecil closed in 1930 after barely thirty-four years' service. The Langham became a home of the BBC in 1946 (although it is now being modernised for use as an hotel again). The Hotel Great Central was bought by the LNER in 1947 for conversion into offices and later the building became British Rail headquarters.

Of the railway hotels, two became war casualties; the Holborn Viaduct Hotel, which had been converted for office use in 1917, was bombed in 1941; the Cannon Street Station Hotel also closed that year after fire bombing. The

Euston Hotel closed prior to demolition in 1963 and the lease on the Craven Hotel was surrendered that same year.

In spite of the intervention of two World Wars, and missed opportunities to modernise, including the failure to incorporate a new hotel in the rebuilding of Euston, the railway hotels have fared well. Five out of the ten still provide a useful service, albeit no longer in railway control since privatisation in 1983.

THE GREAT NORTHERN HOTEL, KING'S CROSS

London's first railway hotels were quite different from one another in their siting and appearance. Philip Hardwick's Euston had a simple elegance, with the twin hotels, the Euston to the right and the Victoria to the left, framing the Doric Arch. At Paddington, his son P.C. Hardwick designed the hotel to stand in front of the train shed. The *Illustrated London News* described the style of the hotel, then well advanced, as 'imitating the French of Louis XIV and later, and the curved roof forms a striking novelty here'.[4]

Lewis Cubitt, who was entrusted with the design of the King's Cross station and hotel, gained his early training under H.E. Kendall (1776–1895); afterwards he worked with his brother Thomas, founder of the well-known building firm. Their early ventures included houses in Eaton Square in the 1820s and in Lowndes Square in 1842. Railway work for Lewis came in 1842–44 with the Bricklayers Arms terminus of the South Eastern Railway and London & Croydon Railway, and the SER's Dover terminus. His preferred Italianate style included useful clock towers at the stations on these lines, a feature employed again as the centrepiece of the King's Cross facade.[5]

When the station opened on 14 October 1852 Mr Edmund Denison, chairman of the company, faced complaints from shareholders concerning the directors' 'extravagance in erecting so splendid a station'. Denison in reply suggested 'that it is the cheapest building for what it contains, and will contain that can be pointed out in London...and that it will not have cost more than £123,500'.[6] He went on to say that the company had still in hand the erection of a hotel at King's Cross at an estimated cost of £30,000.

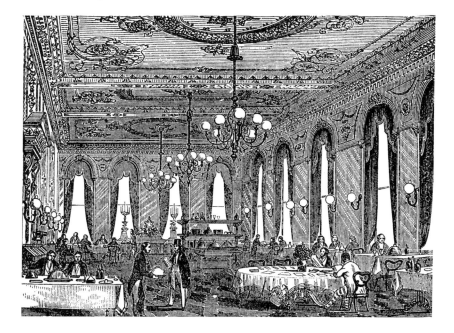

44. The Great Northern Hotel coffee room in its heyday.

45. The Great Northern Hotel, the entrance facade facing across a garden to the station.

The most striking feature of the hotel is its curved plan. This is explained by the earlier topography of the site: the road running north from the New Road towards Camden Town described a distinct curve at its southern end adjacent to the former smallpox hospital. It is clear from maps that when the Great Northern purchased the hospital it inherited a curved site for its future hotel. On the opposite side of the street there were (until the building of St Pancras) terraced houses, so Cubitt designed the hotel to look inwards towards the station across a large garden.

Later, the assertive presence of St Pancras station, with its platform level set some seventeen feet above street level, and projection forward on to Euston Road, took away some of the significance of the Great Northern Hotel in relation to its own station.

A closer look at the Great Northern Hotel reveals that only its six-window wide centre bay is curved and that its outer five-window bays are rectangular in shape. The precedent for the general design is provided by Cubitt's work at Lowndes Square. Both are in a similar Italianate style and have comparable window proportions. The Great Northern has arched heads at ground floor, the Lowndes Square terrace has them at first floor.

To provide relief from the uniformity of the facade, the twin staircase bays at the Great Northern are set slightly forward on the rear elevation, and have fluted pilasters. At the front, these bays have less dominance but the windows are similarly treated with pedimented heads at first and second-floor level, and plainer treatment at third and fourth-floor levels. Built from the same yellow brick as the station the hotel originally had stucco detailing to its window surrounds and cornices altering at each level; however, these have been mutilated, and continuous bands of stucco applied across the heads of the first and second-floor windows. In overall appearance the hotel is not unlike a tall London terrace, five storeys high, with a basement, and a slated roof with attics and high chimneys.

In its internal planning, the hotel was provided with several commendable features. It was one of the first to include rooms on the 'continental system', with bedrooms *en suite* with sitting rooms. Its coffee room, decorated by Crace of Wigmore Street, and measuring 50′ x 30′ rivalled that of the Great Western Royal Hotel as the finest in London. The location of the staircase bays with stone flights, equidistant from each end of the building, aided circulation, and the otherwise apparently endless straight bedroom corridors gained visual relief from the effect of the curved centre bay of the hotel. The company prided itself on the fireproof construction of the hotel, with thick walls dividing every room and with the corridors constructed of brick arches supported by iron girders.

With only one entrance, that in the left-hand stairwell, adjacent to the coffee room, congestion was not uncommon. The introduction of a hydraulic lift in the 1880s lessened the amount of stair climbing to the hotel's one hundred bedrooms. Other changes which have taken place include the building of a basement and ground floor suite of bathrooms and a hairdressing salon, for the benefit of passengers arriving off the nightly sleeping-car trains. Maples also carried out extensive redecorations.[7] Outdoors, the forecourt garden has been swallowed up by extensions to the station and postal services, the area becoming known as 'post-office yard'.

For the first twenty years of its existence, the hotel was leased out before being placed under the control of the GNR's King's Cross Hotel Committee (retitled the Hotels Committee in 1876).[8]

THE MIDLAND GRAND HOTEL

The decision to embark on the huge St Pancras station and hotel project during the early 1860s posed the Midland Railway many problems. On the one hand it hoped to move its headquarters from Derby to London and provide a building which would house both an hotel and offices. On the other financial constraints thwarted the plans and led to delays and significant reductions in the amount of floor space actually built.

The design of the hotel and offices were the subject of an architectural competition, conducted without the guidance of an assessor: the choice of Sir George Gilbert Scott's ambitious entry not only aggravated the situation, but subjected both architect and client to a severe test of confidence. The outcome was a building which took eight years to complete, cost £437,335 and has never ceased to have its critics and admirers. Scott was the architect of over seven hundred projects. Several of his buildings have been in the news recently, including the restoration of the Foreign Office and All Saints, Haley Hill. But it was the design of the Albert Memorial and the Midland Grand Hotel that showed him at his very best.

It was the Midland Railway's desire to be 'on a par with the Great Northern, London and North Western and Great Western' in the provision of hotels,[9] which spurred the company forward. Scott was one of eleven architects invited to enter a competition for the design of the hotel in the summer of 1865. Designs were submitted that autumn and shown at Derby in December. The order of merit, announced in January 1866, was: first, Scott (estimated cost £316,000), second, G. Somers Clarke (£164,000), third, E.M. Barry (£236,487) and fourth, T.C. Sorby (£245,000).[10]

When Scott's plans were accepted in their final form in April 1866, two important alterations were made. For financial reasons two floors of offices were omitted and, with the comfort of visitors in mind, it was decided to include a glazed screen between the end of the train shed and the hotel in an attempt to reduce noise and smoke. In May the collapse of the Overend and Gurney bank and the repercussions of this on the money market, postponed an immediate start on the hotel.

On 5 December Scott met his cliennts with new plans, explaining that these would help reduce costs by about £20,000. These were accepted and he was urged to make economies 'whenever it was practicable to do so'.[11] Two weeks later John Saville was appointed Clerk of Works, at a salary of four guineas a week, to commence his duties on 1 January.[12] The ensuing battle which was to follow centred on Scott's resolution to maintain high standards of finish and his client's desire to reduce expense wherever possible. In May the Board decided that only those parts of the building essential for the completion of the station were to proceed. In December twelve firms submitted tenders but these were to remain unopened for at least a year. Meanwhile, Warings the builders were laying the foundations of the station and hotel.

In March 1868 the Midland Board accepted Jackson and Shaw's tender of £37,580 for the first stage of the work to the hotel.[13] The Board was amenable to Scott's recommendation of Skidmores of Coventry for the supply of gas fittings, but he was rebuked in June 1869 for designing an expensive clock face for the eastern tower. The vital next stage of the work, including the ordering of the eastern tower and fitting out the first part of the hotel, was awarded to Jackson and Shaw at the same rates as those agreed for the earlier contract: a year later they were instructed to proceed with the Great Archway, including the carved work to be undertaken by Farmer and Brindley.[14]

Again the Board were on the look-out for economies. Scott was asked to confer with the Board before ordering internal fittings, and it insisted that its own customers were to be invited to submit tenders for the firegrates and surrounds. Hadens – still a well-known name in engineering – were accepted as central heating installers.

In June 1871 the Board resolved to secure a manager for the hotel, 'by advertisement or otherwise'.[15] The task proved difficult, until Robert Etzensberger was found.[16] He had managed the Victoria Hotel in Venice and been involved in catering on the Nile steamers. The newcomer proved to be a useful ally for Scott, accepting his post on condition that the hotel be completed more or less as originally planned. At an important meeting on 4 June 1872 the Board decided by nine votes to three to confer with their architect about the completion of the hotel. It was decided to complete the entire frontage and two floors only of the curved wing at the western end. Jackson and Shaw were awarded the contract, at 10% on-costs above their 1867 tender prices.

Furnishing of the hotel went on apace with Gillows supplying furniture, Elkingtons the plate and cutlery, Peyton and Peyton the beds, and Sang the decoration. The Midland Grand welcomed its first visitors on 5 May 1873, but arguments still lay ahead. That August, the secretary was instructed to write to Scott insisting that no further expenditure be incurred beyond existing contracts without the assent of the South Construction Committee.[17]

Scott gave the project much personal attention, and in its closing stages his son John Oldrid Scott had the supervision of the decoration of the west wing. In January 1874 their choice of Clayton and Bell for the work was overruled in favour of Gillows.[18] Further arguments centred on the settlement for the final account for stage 1, the proposed heating installation and the use of sculptured figures for the facade. Luckily, completion of the work was in sight: the west wing was finished in June 1876, and on 4 July the whole building was placed in the care of the Way and Works Committee. The final cost of the work disclosed by the chairman to the shareholders in February 1877 was: Fabric £304,335, Decoration and fittings £49,000, Furnishing £84,000, Total £437,335.[19]

Sadly, Scott did not live long enough to see much of his magnificent hotel in

46. Drawing from Scott's office showing the relation between his hotel and the station behind, c1865.

use. In retrospect, he appreciated the Midland Railway's choice of his plans, and spoke of his 'high sense of the honour done in accepting his designs, and the importance of the trust committed to him'.[20] In his *Personal and Professional Recollections*[21] he says that he was persuaded to enter the competition by his friend Joseph Lewis, a Midland Railway director. He drew out his ideas in September 1865, when detained in a small hotel during the illness of one of his sons. He explains how his decision to compete was prompted.'Having been disappointed through Lord Palmerston of my ardent hope of carrying out my style in the Government offices...I was glad to be able to erect one building in that style in London'.

He is here referring to Gothic, and the acrimony of the years 1856–61 when, following his success in the competition for the Government Offices in Whitehall, his Gothic design fell foul of Lord Palmerston, whose insistence on a classical design went against the grain, although Scott acquiesced. However, the tide was turning, for Gothic – as championed by Pugin and Ruskin – came into wide favour during the mid-Victorian period, eventually ousting the Italianate style. In the sphere of hotels, a landmark of its growing popularity was the award of an RIBA gold medal to Ernest George in 1860 for his design for a metropolitan hotel in the Gothic style, 'freely treated and with some continental influence'.[22] Of all commercial buildings in the Gothic style, the Midland Grand is without doubt one of the largest and finest in the world.

Of other hotels built in the Gothic style, the Imperial at Malvern 1862, and the Great Western at Cardiff 1876, are worthy of mention.[23] Although James Fergusson in his *History of the Modern Styles of Architecture* (1873), contrasted the plainness of King's Cross with the 'incongruous medievalism of St Pancras', clearly viewing St Pancras as already out of fashion, others were admirers. For instance, Walford wrote in 1897, 'It stands without rival for palatial beauty, comfort and convenience. The style is a combination of various medieval features, the inspection of which calls to mind the Lombardic and Venetian Brick Gothic, while the critical eye will observe touches of Milan and other Italian terracotta buildings interlaced with good reproduction of details from Winchester and Salisbury Cathedrals and Westminster Abbey. The ornaments from Amiens, Caen and other French edifices. The materials – Gripper's Patent Nottingham bricks with Ancaster stone dressings and shafts of grey and red Peterhead granite.'

One happy feature of the hotel is its harmony with the trainshed, which was already being erected well before work on the hotel began. The trainshed has a slightly pointed apex, and the side walls of the station were already beginning to rise in a characteristic vermillion brick.

Unlike Lewis Cubitt, who had little established precedent for hotel planning to draw upon, Scott's schedule of accommodation, which was of his own making, drew from the growing number of London hotels, including the Grosvenor and the Langham. The latest technology was available too, in the design of hydraulic lifts, central heating, bathroom and kitchen planning, and fire-resistant construction. The *Building News* outlined the accommodation at the Midland Grand.'The ground floor east of the departure gateway [the left hand arch], consists of the entrance hall, staircase and rooms devoted to general management…and lifts, also to refreshment and dining rooms. The east end of the arrival gateway [the right hand arch] has four large rooms set aside for station purposes. A basement extends under this portion. The [curved] West Wing embraces the general public entrance with a covered carriage way…leading to a spacious vestibule; the coffee room…with circular ends; the grand staircase, and the rear of this wing is appropriated to casual visitors, and comprises billiard and smoking rooms and toilets. At the extreme rear are the laundry, drying rooms, with wash houses and engine room below. In the basement under the West Wing is the kitchen and servants' offices. The first floor is sitting and bedrooms, the chief feature is a ladies' reading room, and dining room over the entrance, in the rear billiard rooms etc., in all fifty two rooms on this floor. The second, third and fourth floors are all available for letting purposes in sitting and bedrooms'.[24]

Currently, amid the faded splendour of the rooms, many of them sub-divided by partitioning, it is difficult to appreciate what the decorations and colour schemes looked like. M.D. Conway, an American visitor in 1882, had this to say: '…it has been decorated by Robert Sang and furnished by Gillow, in the most expensive style and certainly presents some rich interiors. The reading room has green cloth wallpaper, and a ceiling gay with huge leaf frescoes. It is divided by a double arch with gilded architraves. The mantle pieces are dark maple with two small pillars of yellow marble set on either side. The coffee room has a general tone of drab with touches of gold in the paper, and a sort of sarcophagus chimney piece surmounted by an antique mirror of bevelled glass. The sitting room has floral paper and a imitation mosaic ceiling. One of the bedrooms has deep green wallpaper with gold lines and spots, and bed curtains somewhat similar. The halls and corridors have a dado of fine dark brown tile and bright fleur-de-lis paper above.'[25]

Following the opening of the hotel, inevitable teething troubles occurred. A malfunction of the passenger lift supplied by Sir William Armstrong caused temporary concern.[26] Traffic noise from cabs passing under both archways was remedied with the help of rubber strips inserted in wood block paving.[27] Wood blocks were similarly substituted for the granite setts in the Euston Road.[28] Such care for detail was typical.

WILLIAM TOWLE AND THE MIDLAND GRAND
Although St Pancras never became headquarters of the Midland Railway, it was home of its Hotels, Refreshment Room and Restaurant Car Department,

47. *Ladies' sitting room, above the main entrance of the Midland Grand Hotel.*

followed by LMS Hotels and British Transport Hotels, spanning in all the years 1884–1983. For the first sixty years of this period the Department was run by the Towle family. Sir William (1849–1929) moved to St Pancras from Derby in 1884, and was joined by his sons Francis William (1876–1951) and Arthur Edward (1878–1949) as joint assistant managers in 1898; they succeeded him as Joint Managers in 1914. Francis later became Managing Director of Gordon Hotels in 1921, and Arthur became controller of LMS Hotels until his retirement in 1944. Hence, the Towle family itself was an important part of the hotel's history.

When Sir William retired, G. Murray Smith, chairman of the Midland Railway, said, 'We regret to lose Mr Towle's services, which have been of the very

48. A typical sitting room in the Midland Grand as furnished by Gillows.

greatest value to the Midland company, and have placed this company in the premier position among railways in the excellence of its hotels, dining cars and refreshment rooms.'[29]

William Towle was an innovator. He introduced luncheon baskets for passengers at Derby during the 1870s and provided the first restaurant cars for third class ticket holders. His talent had already been recognised when, in 1884, he succeed Robert Etzensberger at the Midland Grand. The following year he was given charge of the Queen's Hotel, Leeds, too. He later masterminded the building or acquisition of hotels at Bradford in 1890, Liverpool in 1892, Heysham in 1896, Keighley in 1902, and Manchester in 1903; he also supervised the rebuilding of the Adelphi, Liverpool, which was completed in the year of his retirement, 1914.

His success stemmed from his attention to detail or 'personality of direction'.[30] From his headquarters at St Pancras he visited each of the principal hotels weekly and the other hotels and about forty refreshment rooms frequently.

In 1893, his ability as controller was recognised in that his salary, which had hitherto been £1500 per annum and on a par with other heads of department, was adjusted to take into account a 4% commission on the profits made by his department. With a gross profit of £55,213 less expenses, his salary rose to £2673[31] in accordance with normal practice. This included his wife's services in supervising housekeeping and female staff.

49. The coffee room on the ground floor of the Midland Grand.

Towle's care for detail is illustrated by a series of memoranda to staff that survive.[32] The topics they cover include quality control in the making of soup, recipes on how to mix cold Bovril and soda, cleanliness, complaints about smoking, injunctions to turn off the gas before closing a kitchen, and a reminder for staff that instant dismissal awaited those found guilt of serving up the accumulated dregs from opened bottles.

The culinary and managerial expertise of foreign nationals was much sought after. Towle's predecessor, Etzensberger, and Charles Schumann, manager of the Great Northern Hotel, both served tough apprenticeships before coming to Britain. Mr A. Pardini, who managed the Great Northern Hotel in the 1950s before moving to the Euston, got his first job in Britain as a waiter at the Midland Grand in 1922. As a fourteen-year-old he had worked a twelve-hour day without pay for his first six months at the Grand Hotel, Marseilles.

Life behind the scenes at the Midland Grand left fond memories with P.W. Smith of Bedford, who began work as a fifteen-year-old page in 1898. He had seen an advertisement which read: 'Wanted, boys for Railway Refreshment rooms and Hotels. Apply Head Office, Midland Grand Hotel, St Pancras Station, London.' A free pass took him to London, followed by a successful interview and the beginning of a career that lasted fifty-eight years. He served five employers, the Midland Railway, Frederick Hotels, the LMS, the LNER and Trust House. At the Midland Grand he wore a chocolate coloured uniform with brass buttons, worked a thirteen-hour day, took meals when there was spare time, and received two and sixpence (13p) a week. There was little time off, one half day one week, alternating with all day off the following Sunday. The head chef, a Frenchman named Albert, helped guests to enjoy his exquisite cuisine by introducing a small orchestra, an unusual feature at that time. Nearby was the ladies' smoking room, equipped with an electrophone which linked guests by telephone line to the Queen's Hall and other London halls and churches. Another room had a column printer that relayed news from the Stock Exchange, and racing results.

There were occasions when a page could rise to a position of importance. In 1899 the Van Kannel Door Co. were trying to interest the British market in their revolving door, and sold a set to the Midland Grand. Smith got the job of demonstrating the door to the local fire officer, and earned a tip. Treats and the occasional outing were organised by the National Sunday League with visits to Boulogne and other cross-Channel ports. Discipline at work was strict. Smith recalled two written reprimands: 'Please note that you will be fined threepence for eating an apple on duty', and, 'Please note that you will be fined sixpence for being in your bedroom while on duty'. He was later transferred to dining cars and then back to the Midland Grand for a spell as a porter, receptionist and lift man, before leaving the hotel for good in 1912.[33]

Two friends, Reg Squires and Stan Humphrey, both began as pages at the Midland Grand in 1912 and 1914 respectively. The hotel employed eight pages and their pay was three shillings and sixpence (18p) per week). Squires saw the Midland Grand close in 1935 and thereafter was one of three porters detailed to meet the St Pancras trains in an attempt to steer guests to the Euston Hotel, and not to the rival Great Northern.[34]

PUBLICITY, PROFITS AND TARIFFS

Soon after the opening of the Great Northern Hotel at Easter 1854, a price list was issued. The hotel is shown in a rural setting with trees and shrubs and no hint of the adjacent station. An attractive sketch of the Coffee Room shows the room set with the customary large tables of the period and the decorations carried out by Crace.[35]

Lifts were at first unusual.[36] Before the wider introduction of vertical railways, ascending chambers and rising or lifting rooms, as the first lifts were called, visitors were reluctant to pay much for rooms above the first two or three floors. This is reflected in the Great Northern's price list. Guests had to be on the look out for extras too, because a coal fire in the bedroom cost one shilling (5p), wax lights one shilling and sixpence (8p), and a hot bath two shillings (10p), which doubled the bill.

The prices listed were less than those charged at the Victoria and Euston at their opening fourteen years earlier. Euston charged five shillings (25p) for accommodation on the first floor, four shillings (20p) for the second and third floor and three shillings and sixpence (18p) for the fourth floor. Breakfast cost two shillings and sixpence (13p). When the Euston closed 123 years later, a single-bed room cost £1.17.6d (188p) and £2.17.6d (288p) with a private bath. Breakfast cost four shillings (20p).

The Great Northern's tariff in 1989 is £50 for a single room without a bath, £70 with a bath, £65 for a twin or double without a bath and £85 with, full English breakfast included. Egon Ronay, writing on the subject of rising costs, observed that charges have risen out of all recognition during the past thirty years, yet 'customers seem to have accepted higher prices with remarkably little resistance'.

In 1879 Charles Dickens jnr. published the *Dickens Directory of London*. Foreign visitors were advised that 'the continental custom of taking all or the majority of meals out of the hotel does not obtain in England, and that a London hotel keeper under such circumstances will consider himself ill-used.

50. *The grand staircase at the Midland Grand. Here as elsewhere Scott was content to leave his structural ironwork fully exposed.*

Attendance is now usually included in the bill. When this is the case the servants invariably expect very much the same gratuity as when it was not included.'

The inclusive charges per person, per day, for bedroom, breakfast with coffee and cold meat, dinner with soup and joint, attendance etc., were eleven shillings and sixpence (58p) at the Euston, twelve shillings and sixpence (63p) at the Grosvenor, thirteen shillings and sixpence (68p) at the Great Western Royal, and fourteen shillings (70p) at the Midland Grand and the Great Northern. In the non-railway sector, the Westminster Palace charged the equivalent of 63p and the Langham 73p.

Illustrations of the Midland Grand, one of the most photogenic of buildings, appeared in the Midland Railway's Official Guides, on letter headings, advertisements, timetables and tariffs. William Towle's arrival at the hotel in 1884 was soon followed by a new approach to proclaiming its excellence. A full-page advertisement in the 1888 edition of *Whitaker's Almanac* shows the hotel almost elevationally, and with five floors, in accordance with Scott's original plans. Towle was at pains to advise customers that the hotel could meet 'the requirements of those who desire the most sumptuous apartments, or a modest bachelor's bedroom; and a cuisine and wine list will be found to embrace the elegance of the French Cuisine, and the choicest vintages, and the simplest meals with the wine of the Gironde, or the Rhone at one shilling the half bottle'. Innovations included electric light, telegraph and telephone to theatres and business centres. Table d'hôte open to non-residents was one of Frederick Gordon's innovations at his Grand Hotel, Northumberland Avenue, when it opened in 1881, and this was copied by Towle.

The introduction of picture postcards in the first years of this century was a useful form of advertising. The Great Northern Railway and Midland Railway both issued several sets of cards featuring their hotels: the Great Northern was shown along with its namesakes at Bradford, Leeds and Scarborough. A now rare and unusual card issued by the Midland Railway in about 1910 doubled as a tariff for the Midland Grand. It featured a fine easterly view of the hotel and drew attention to the new two and sixpenny (13p) luncheon on offer in the magnificent dining room, where Herr Dresher's Viennese Orchestra played. Emphasis too was given to the highest class cuisine and exquisite restaurant and lounge on the first floor.

An important outlet for hotel advertisements were guide books which frequently included reference to both the Great Northern and the Midland Grand hotels. In 1912 the former was listed in Bradshaw's guide as a 'High class family hotel; quiet and convenient situation; with well appointed rooms, electric light, recherché cuisine, and lifts to all floors.' Its telephone number was 3543 North and its telegraphic address was 'NORTHNESS'. The same issue of Bradshaw's featured a south-westerly perspective view of the Midland Grand, claimed to be 'London's most comfortable hotel'; its famous MIDOTEL telegraphic address was included.

There were also guide books to London published abroad. The first of Baedeker's famous guides came out in 1854, just as the Great Western Royal and the Great Northern hotels were opening. Baedeker prided himself on the accuracy of his information and his publishing house was the first to award star ratings to objects, views and hotels. Two stars were only granted to such masterpieces as the Louvre, St Peter's, Rome and the Pyramids. A sample of Baedeker's attention to detail and up-to-date information comes from the London guide (18th edition) for 1923, which itemised such modern luxuries as electric light, lifts, central heating, ample bath accommodation, telephones in bedrooms and in many cases, private orchestras.

In central London and its environs, nearly one hundred and thirty hotels were listed, twenty eight of which were starred. Of the railway hotels, only the

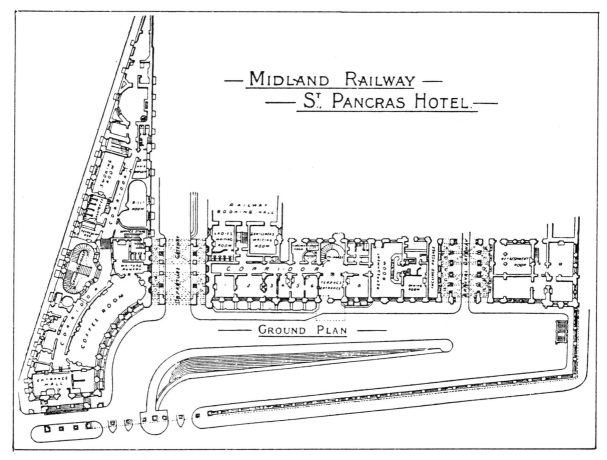

51. Ground floor plan of the Midland Grand Hotel. The layout, though magnificent in its architectural effect, made the hotel difficult to run.

Midland Grand and the Great Eastern at Liverpool Street were considered worthy of such a rating. The tariffs listed for 1923 included the Cannon Street at nineteen and sixpence (98p) for bed, breakfast, lunch and dinner, the Midland Grand at £1.2.0d (110p), with a surcharge of seven and sixpence (38p) for a room with *en suite* bathroom, and the Euston at £1.2.6d (113p).

Helped by such publicity, the hotels flourished though, in the competitive business of hotel management, little was divulged about the precise profits earned by the Midland Grand and the Great Northern hotels. In 1889, for example, a shareholder was told by M.W. Thompson, Chairman of the Midland Railway, that their hotels paid, but that he was not prepared to disclose any details of their working and management.[37] By 1893, with William Towle firmly in control of their hotels, a profit of £55,200 was recorded.

The Midland Grand enjoyed its golden years up to the outbreak of World War One. When the Midland became part of the LMS Railway, profits at the Midland Grand for 1925 were £15,845, which compared with £15,418 earned at the Euston, but fell far short of the £85,007 earned by the Midland Hotel, Manchester. Hard times in 1931–3 reduced profits to four figures, and in 1934, the year before its closure, the Midland Grand's profits were barely £2781 compared with £7039 at Euston and £50,579 at the Midland, Manchester.[38]

CONCLUSION

Of the railway hotels in general, Sir William Towle observed, 'The nation owes a great debt of gratitude to the railway companies for the provision of many good hotels which would certainly never have been built by other capital.'[39]

Almost one hundred and forty were built or purchased. It was inevitable that some would be demolished to make way for modernisation, like the famous Euston and the Queen's, Birmingham. About twenty-three have gone, thirty-four more have changed their use, but seventy-nine still serve their original purpose, sure confirmation of their validity. The recent restoration and modernisation of the Gleneagles Hotel, Perthshire, the Caledonian, Edinburgh and the Midland, Manchester, are just three examples of famous railway-built hotels going forward with confidence into the twenty-first century.

Doubt exists over the future of the Great Northern Hotel in the light of the Channel Tunnel terminus debate, despite its continuous successful history as a hotel for nearly 150 years. The Midland Grand, on the other hand, has experienced an appropriately dramatic history. Closed, as we have seen, in 1935, it was then converted to offices. In 1977, in the context of rumours of the hotel's reopening, a cleaning and restoration programme began, but this was halted in 1980 for financial reasons. Finally, after years of indecision, the Midland Grand is poised for a new career, following the granting of conditional planning consent to a consortium partnered by the British Railways Board, Speyhawk plc and Sir Robert McAlpine & Sons Ltd.[40] The consent includes provision for refurbishment, and change of use from offices and hotel, to part hotel, club, retail shops, restaurant and flats. All in all, it seems set for a bright future.

FOOTNOTES

1 17 September 1853.
2 Public Record Office, LMS Hotels Committee, Minute 1659.
3 P. Boniface, *Hotels and Restaurants 1830 to Present Day*, (HMSO 1981).
4 December 1852.
5 A three bell chiming clock was in use 1852–1914, 1924–27.
6 C.H. Grinling, *History of the GNR*, (1924).
7 PRO Rail 236/192.
8 PRO King's Cross Hotel Committee, 11 June 1874, held at King's Cross.
9 *Railway Times*, 1868, p52.
10 *The Builder*, 1865, p896; 1866, p33.
11 PRO Midland 1/19 Minute 7157.
12 PRO Midland 1/279 Minute 453.
13 Minute 753.
14 Minutes 1188, 1204, 1210, 1215, 1300.
15 PRO Midland 1/20 Minute 8707.
16 Midland 1/280 Minute 1396.
17 Midland 1/281 Minute 1511.
18 Midland 1/281 Minutes 1536/6, 1544/5, 1629/50, 1747/74/81, 1812/26.
19 Midland 1/9 66th Half-yearly meeting, 20 Feb 1877.
20 Midland 1/19 Minute 6914.
21 Edited by his eldest son, 1879.
22 *Illustrated London News*, 7 Jan 1860.
23 Not railway owned.
24 *Building News*, 1874 p554, 558, 559.
25 *Travels in South Kensington*, (New York 1882).
26 Midland 1/28 Minute 1718/32/38.
27 Minute 1935/57.
28 Midland 1/274 Minutes 46/58.
29 *Railway Gazette*, March 1914, p390.
30 *Railway Magazine*, April 1916, p245.
31 PRO Midland Railway Hotel Committee, 14 June 1894.
32 PRO Rail 1022/3 XK 1991.
33 *Railway Observer*, 1964–5.
34 *Chronicle*, April 1963.
35 Official illustrated *Guide to the Great Northern Railway*.
36 One of the first hotels to incorporate a lift was the Grosvenor at Victoria Station.
37 91st meeting of Shareholders, 9 August 1889.
38 BTH records.
39 *Railway News*, Jubilee Edition, 1914.
40 23 February 1989.

CHAPTER FIVE

King's Cross Goods Yard

Robert Thorne
with Stephen Duckworth and Barry Jones

Goods traffic is the Cinderella of railway history. Though it is customary to acknowledge that the lines which pioneered the English railway system were intended primarily for freight, that ancestry has only marginally influenced the study of how the system subsequently evolved. Passengers were also carried on some of the early lines, and it was the novelty and glamour of that traffic, not to mention its profitability, which stole the show: in much the same way, it has continued to steal the attention of historians ever since. The chronicle of railway development, as it has popularly been told, celebrates the introduction of progressively faster passenger trains, running to increasingly far-flung destinations. By contrast goods traffic, mundane and slow, has seemed far less captivating. Only economic historians, interested in aggregate figures of what was carried and how well it paid, have put freight in the leading position it deserves.

The dearth of interest in goods traffic may be partly related to the element of personal memory in the writing of railway history. Many accounts of the passenger side of railway operations rely on their authors' own recollections and likewise their popularity often stems from a sense of shared nostalgia with their readership. Almost everyone over a certain age has a fund of evocative memories of train journeys to draw upon. The same background of collective experience hardly exists where freight is concerned. For although most people can recall a time when freight trains were far more common than they are now, that aspect of the railways was always far less public. Goods handling represented a separate realm, with its own buildings and staff, and its own peculiar hours of work. In particular, railway goods yards were secret enclaves, walled off from the world outside and guarded like barracks or naval dockyards. Only since the decline of goods traffic have the yards become more accessible, enabling historians to redeem their previous neglect of that part of the story.

Of course the recent opportunities that have emerged for the study of railway goods handling have been double-edged in their effect. It has been immensely exciting to be able to explore and record part of the railway system that had previously been beyond public bounds, but that chance has come because of a decline of business which erased one important aspect of the subject. Because in most goods yards the trains have gone, and the rails have been taken up, many details of daily operations have been lost. They may be recalled by those who once worked in the yards, but hearing even the most

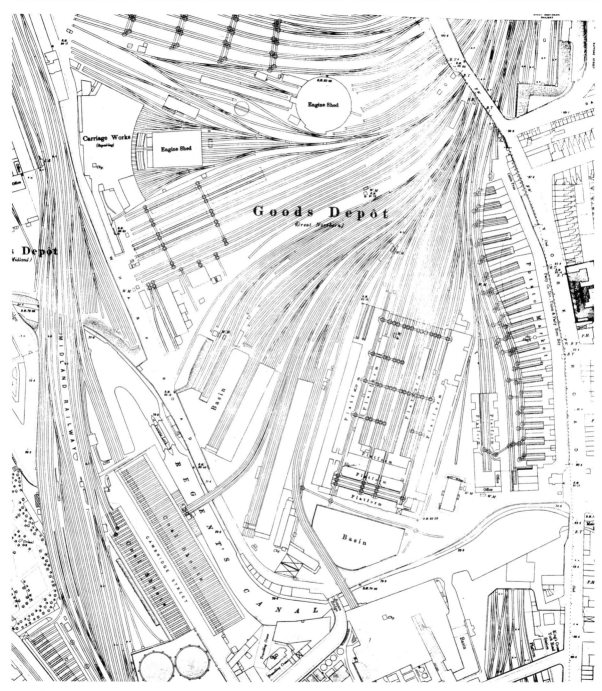

52. The King's Cross goods yard as it was in 1894, just before the western goods shed was added.

detailed reminiscence is no substitute for seeing the actual activity. For the most part the study of goods handling, because it has been taken up so late, has had to be mainly archaeological. That is why this essay is largely devoted to the analysis of buildings, and only secondarily to the processes they once housed. In better circumstances that order of priorities might well have been reversed.

Though it is galling not to have been able to record the goods yard at King's Cross in the full flood of activity, there is enough evidence in the buildings that remain, and in archival documents, to suggest that the site is one of the most important of its kind. At the outset it was developed with ambitious aims, both regarding the traffic it would deal with and how it would be handled. The Great Northern Railway served some of the richest farming areas in the country, from market gardens just north of London to the wheatfields of Lincolnshire, all of which it could link to metropolitan markets through King's Cross. The fish trade from Hull, Grimsby and the northeast also came within its sphere. Before the coming of the railways the effect of London's insatiable appetite had been felt hundreds of miles away. The increasing popularity of potatoes as a supplement to working class diet was partly answered by supplies brought by sea from Lincolnshire, and there was also a sea-borne trade in cattle from Scotland. The railways helped stimulate demand by improving the speed and regularity of supply, and in the case of more perishable fruit and vegetables they helped widen the area in which cultivation for the London market was possible.

Foodstuffs, plus regular goods, would have been enough for many railways, but King's Cross dealt with another major commodity as well. In the battle to wrest the coal supply of London from sea-borne carriers the GNR led the way, primarily by exploiting alternative sources in South Yorkshire but also by attacking the heartland of the sea traders in the north east. At first most of the coal that the GNR handled came through specially-designed drops at King's Cross.

At its peak of activity the King's Cross yard included 59 acres of warehouses, sheds, stables, offices and sidings. What is remarkable is how much of that world has survived. Although most of the sidings have gone, and the engine shed ('Top Shed' of steam age fame) has been demolished, most of the first generation of GNR buildings are still standing, plus many of their successors. The only key element, apart from the railway tracks, that is missing is the link to the Regent's Canal. The original development provided for the smooth transfer of goods from railway to canal and vice versa by running two canal basins into the yard, one in front of the main goods warehouses with branches into the buildings, and the other serving coal and stone wharves. The fact that these have long been filled in makes it harder, though not impossible, to understand why mid-Victorian observers were so excited by the arrangement of the site. But even without the basins it is easy to appreciate their feeling that, through this enterprising development, the Great Northern had revolutionised the supply of key commodities to London.

Amongst the first generation of main line railways built in London, only the London and Birmingham (or the London and North Western as it became) established a goods yard of a similar scale. Its site in Camden also permitted transhipment to the Regent's Canal via links which can still be clearly seen, but its whole operation was less ambitious than the Great Northern's: in particular, it did not covet the coal trade to quite the same extent. The Camden yard, even in its dismembered state, would merit further study and recording. As things stand, only Bricklayers Arms yard in south London has been studied at the same level of historical detail as King's Cross.[1]

In terms of location, the yards at Camden, King's Cross and elsewhere in London all have one thing in common: they are all some distance from their allied passenger termini. Land costs in Victorian cities, especially London, were such that no railway company could dream of establishing its goods facilities alongside its main line terminus except in special circumstances. And quite apart from the expense of such land-hungry developments, there were legitimate operational reasons for segregating passenger and goods traffic. So while every effort was made to bring passengers as close to the heart of the city as possible, goods traffic was generally siphoned off a mile or so further out, where yards could sprawl expansively.

At King's Cross, these customary priorities were almost thrown into reverse. The site for the goods yard was an obvious one, and the principal dilemma for the directors was whether they could afford to fulfill the passenger station aspect of their ambitions. It was often said that the last half mile was the most expensive part of any route into London: for the Great Northern, in addition to land costs, there were also daunting engineering problems in reaching their final destination.

Before the Great Northern, or any of its precursor schemes, had been thought of, the land behind the present King's Cross Station had been dissected by the Regent's Canal, opened in 1820. As Alan Faulkner explains in Chapter Two, the canal was an attractive location for industrial development and warehouses, especially where it ran through parts of the urban fringes that had already been colonised for such uses. Seen through the eyes of Reginald Wilfer in *Our Mutual Friend*, the area was a semi-industrial twilight zone: 'a tract of suburban Sahara, where tiles and bricks were burnt, bones were boiled, rubbish was shot, dogs fought, and dust was heaped by contractors.'[2] Most of these activities could be moved elsewhere – even the dust heaps were transitory – with the exception of the tileworks. Randell's tileworks, to the north of the canal off Maiden Lane (later York Way), were not directly affected by the advent of the railway, but other kilns had to make way for the tracks entering the goods yard. South of the canal, apparently beyond Mr Wilfer's range of observation, were the conspicuous works of the Imperial Gas Company. Their demand for fuel was sufficient to merit a special canal basin for deliveries, just as subsequently the railway provided a separate bridge into the works for coal that came by train.

The site of the future goods yard, opposite the gas works on the north bank of the canal, was free of permanent buildings, so there was no logical reason why its developement could not have been started soon after the railway was sanctioned in 1846. Other parts of the line, parcelled out to various contractors, went ahead but the southernmost section, let to the contractor John Jay in 1848, hung fire in a tantalising way. That was not his fault: the main problem, as with so many metropolitan schemes, was one of finalising the land purchases. There were not many proprietors to deal with, but on the site of the intended passenger station there were two hospitals and negotiations over their acquisition (including the removal of one of them to a new site in Islington) delayed work on the whole final section of the line. Figures which the Great Northern later released showed that its land and compensation costs for the stretch between King's Cross and Hornsey were by far the highest for any section of the route to York.[3]

Negotiations over land not only had the effect of delaying the start of John Jay's contract: early in 1849 it looked as if they might result in the passenger station part of his assignment being dropped altogether. It was always recognised that the final approach to the terminus, involving a tunnel under the Regent's Canal, would be one of the hardest bits of construction on the line. That difficulty, plus the cost of the station site, brought about a change of heart amongst those who previously had advocated the Euston Road as the only feasible place for the terminus. If, as had been calculated, a saving of up to £400,000 could be made by stopping north of the canal it might be reasonable to accommodate passenger trains in the goods yard, even though that would not

53. The Granary: Lewis Cubitt's watercolour perspective as exhibited at the Royal Academy in 1851.

54. The third floor of the Granary. Low floor heights were no disadvantage in traditional warehousing.

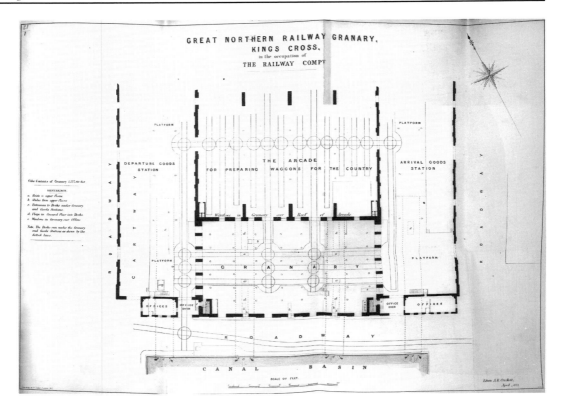

55. An 1873 plan of the Granary and transit sheds, showing the track and turntable layouts.

be a very appealing location for travellers. William Cubitt, consulting engineer to the Great Northern, was horrified at the thought of cancelling the most prestigious part of the whole project and fought for the directors' agreement that, if such a solution to the company's troubles were adopted, it would be only as a temporary measure. So it was decided to include short-term passenger facilities in the goods yard, inconvenient though they might be, and to postpone construction of the terminus. But for the sake of engineering convenience, and as a sign of good intent, work on the tunnel leading to the permanent station was sanctioned at the same time.[4]

Once Jay had started to prepare the site the directors appointed Lewis Cubitt (the nephew of their consulting engineer) as architect for the necessary buildings, including the temporary station, the goods warehouses and offices, and the engine sheds. His drawings were ready by January 1850, except apparently for those relating to the Granary.[5] A set dated March 1850, which he subsequently presented to the library of the Institution of Civil Engineers, still show no sign of the Granary but there is no doubt that it was conceived of as part of the original scheme and that though delayed, work on it started during the same year. The temporary station was ready for opening in August 1850, and the first freight trains left the yard a few months later. The Granary and coal drops were brought into use in 1851.[6]

When Cubitt presented his drawings he emphasised that in his opinion 'all the buildings should be erected in a plain, substantial manner.'[7] That, no doubt, was exactly what the directors wanted to hear, for architectural flamboyance was not what they would have expected to find in a goods yard. Yet, as he was soon to show in his designs for King's Cross station, an element of

56. Queen Victoria leaving for Scotland from the temporary terminus at King's Cross in 1851.

austerity could be turned to dramatic effect. There was enough inherent grandeur in the functions of the goods yard to permit a degree of heroics while still keeping safely within the bounds of plainness. Above all the site, as seen from a lower level further south, with the canal as its pedestal, could be composed as an industrial acropolis dominated by its warehouses. However purposefully inoffensive his first comments may have been, Cubitt never thought that bare functionalism need be self-effacing. The watercolour of the Granary and sheds which he exhibited at the Royal Academy in 1851 suggests that, quite the contrary, he viewed the site in the noblest architectural terms.

An examination of what the goods yard looked like when it first opened can best start with that familiar sight of the Granary. Today's view differs form the watercolour perspective in two main respects: the canal basin, which provides the picture with such an animated foreground, has been filled in and two three-storey office buildings, flanking the Granary, obscure the end elevations of the transit sheds. The picture records what is now much harder to appreciate about this commanding layout – the way in which the Granary and its adjoining sheds were integrated as a functional totality. Although the sheds were finished first, space was left for the Granary to rise between them as the culmination of the goods yard group. Both sheds and Granary were entered by canal branches from the basin, and in that sense were equals, but the hipped ends of the sheds were set back in deference to the Granary's superior status.

The Granary, today as when first built, is six storeys high, rising to a prominent cornice which hides a double-hipped roof. Its long main facade is broken up by four slightly projecting bays, like giant Doric pilasters, incorporating stacks of hoist openings. Tiers of arch-headed windows fill the intermediate bays. Like the best of similar buildings of its time – the Albert Dock in Liverpool or Jarrolds' printing works in Norwich, for example – it makes no attempt at superfluous effect, relying instead on the muted expression of its purpose. Cubitt and his contemporaries were used to employing a stretched or diluted classicism in domestic and street architecture, but when applied at this much larger scale it was harder to maintain its meaning. In that regard the Granary is a notable success.

Inside, functional requirements take absolute precedence. The primary internal structure is cast iron but timber is far more evident than might be

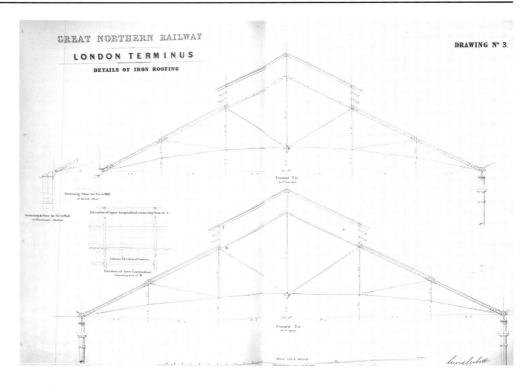

57. *A Lewis Cubitt drawing of the roof trusses for the temporary passenger terminus.*

58. *Digging Gasworks Tunnel in 1852. The spoil was removed via a temporary wooden viaduct into the Goods Yard.*

expected. Cast iron columns and beams are used on every floor, the columns getting progressively smaller in circumference on the way up. On all except the top floor the columns support two parallel beams spanning each bay, on the bottom flanges of which rest subsidiary timber beams, and from these spring the transverse joists of the floors above. As a structural system this holds few surprises, except that the columns and beams appear to be fixed by nothing more than the weight of material they carry. On the top floor the system changes so as to support the roof trusses plus, at one time, wrought iron water tanks that were used as reservoirs for fire-fighting. The two roofs, with a broad valley gutter between them, run the length of the granary on timber queen post trusses, bracketed and tied with iron. On the outer walls these trusses are supported on stone corbels, but down the centre of the building they rest on columns and beams similar to those on the floors below. The other columns on the same floor are shorter and carry correspondingly deeper beams to which, on the only occasion in the whole building, they are fastened by bolts. These more robust bays must have been designed for the water tanks, now long since removed.

It has become customary to assess buildings such as the Granary largely in terms of technical innovation; to place them in a line of succession in which the increasingly sophisticated use of iron, and later steel, is their main claim to merit. Looked at in that way the Granary cannot be rated very highly. In the half century before it was built structural advances, particularly in the design of textile mills, had brought the use of iron framing into common practice. From the pioneering work of William Strutt and Charles Bage at the end of the eighteenth century the design of ironwork, especially the size and dimension of beams, had been gradually refined, allowing timber to be banished from buildings where the risk of fire was the chief anxiety. By the 1840s it was usual for the mills of Lancashire and Yorkshire to have cast iron circular columns carrying I-beams from which sprang solid or hollow brick arches: the roof trusses would be cast or wrought iron, or possibly a combination of the two.[8] But what was thought essential in the design of a mill, where inflammable fibres would be handled alongside running machinery, was less important in a warehouse building, especially one using hydraulic and manual power for lifting, because there seemed no pressing reason to do otherwise, and the survival of the building with almost all its fabric intact has proved his point. Its intended purpose called for no great innovation of the kind that other struc-tures required, but the result was none the worse for that.

The ground floor of the Granary was designed to be considerably higher than the other floors to allow headroom for handling goods brought in by canal and railway. The differing levels on the site meant that in fact the two docks which ran from the canal basin into the Granary entered at basement level, and were reached by openings in the floor which could be closed when not in use. Nothing of that intriguing system survives today. Tracks also came into the building, through openings in both the side and rear walls, and waggons could be turned on two sets of turntables in the loading bay area.

Whereas the Granary was designed to look south, the railway tracks were a reminder that most of its life-blood came from the other direction. This was even more true for the transit sheds which flanked it and the huge train assembly shed which filled the space to its rear. The transit sheds also incorpo-rated canal docks, but they were both much more dependent on railway tracks which, entering at the north end, ran the whole of their 580ft length. These tracks served central platforms, on the opposite side of which were the road-ways for carting goods in an out. This tripartite function, as applied to the eastern (arrivals) shed, can be clearly seen in the Cubitt watercolour. And the sheds were put to even more uses than was at first apparent, for under each of their platforms stabling was provided for about 75 horses, reached by ramps from the roadways.[9]

Seen from outside the transit sheds are simple brick structures, with blank segmental arches punctuating their majestic length. Inside, their platforms and tracks have been removed, and their original wooden roof trusses have been replaced in steel. The space between them was designed to have twelve tracks on which waggons brought from the transit sheds or the Granary with the aid of turntables, could be assembled into trains. Cubitt's drawings of March 1850 showed this area only partly roofed, but the specification anticipated its complete roofing before very long. The finished roof had four bays, each of 45ft span, with the tracks evenly divided between them.[10] Today the space is still the same – all the more dramatic now that it is empty – but most of the roof has been replaced with steel trusses on rolled steel columns. After so many changes in the transit sheds and the train assembly area it is a surprise to have discovered, as the inventory indicates, that part of the original roof has survived in a transposed location.

Those who entered the goods yard in its first year of operation, particularly if they were going to catch a train from the temporary passenger station, would have seen the Granary and the transit sheds from the Maiden Lane gateway, but their attention would have been drawn first of all to three other buildings grouped nearer to the entrance road. The furthest away of these was the goods office, described by Cubitt with typical reserve as 'a plain common Brick Building'.[11] As an office block, completed when purpose-built examples of its kind were rare, its huge windows and convenient plan were admirable; and in its recently transformed state as Regeneration House it has continued to serve its purpose well. Next to it was the carriage shed, known for most of its life as the Midland Shed because the Midland Railway leased it in 1857 at the outset of its short-lived experiment of using the Great Northern's London facilities. The full history of this building is something of an archaeological nightmare since it appears to have been altered a dozen or more times. As built, it was a shed capable of holding (it was said) 80 carriages, and was presumably single-storeyed.[12] Either during the Midland Railway's occupancy or soon after, it had a storey added, but this has since been altered and reroofed. Even with its two tracks removed it is possible to imagine how the ground floor was used (though the turntable arrangements are tantalisingly ghostly); but the single uninterrupted space of the upper floor, with its twentieth century steel truss roof, hides as much as it reveals.

Closest to Maiden Lane was the temporary passenger station, the staggered curves of its platforms looking on plan like a broken jug handle. As with most early main line termini (including King's Cross when it was first brought into use) the emphasis was on the departure side. Passengers for the north would pass through a station building containing the booking office before boarding their train under a 500ft long iron and glass roof. Arriving passengers, on the other hand, came in under an adjacent roof that was just as long but was slid back beyond the end of the departure shed and had no building allotted to it. When Queen Victoria departed for Scotland in August 1851 – quite a coup for the newly-opened line – she appears to have been provided with a special platform in the arrival shed. The *Illustrated London News* artist who recorded the scene quite understandably had difficulty in depicting the curved configuration of roofs as they stretched away to the north, but in matters of engineering detail he was commendable careful. Both roofs were triangulated, with raised central louvres. They had composite rafters of wood encased in wrought iron plate, supported by wrought iron struts and ties. The slightly arched bottom tie was connected to the central strut and two diagonals by an ornamental boss, the hallmark of that kind of truss as used on the site.[13]

Considering that they were intended to be short-lived, the roofs of the temporary passenger station have shown a dogged refusal to disappear.

Although the trusses have gone, many of the spandrel beams which linked the bays of the roof have survived: eighteen of them as part of a later roof alongside the Midland Shed, on the same curved line as the boundary of the passenger station, and four embedded in the remains of the potato market. As fragments of one of the earliest stations in London these beams deserve to be better known.

The other parts of the original goods yard were beyond the Granary and its canal basin, where only those on business would have reason to venture. First and foremost there were the eastern coal drops, running like a Roman aqueduct into the heart of the site. These, and the slightly later western coal drops, form part of the coal trade story that is dealt with in Chapter Six. At the southern end of both sets of drops the road through the site ran on a curved viaduct, in the arches of which stables were inserted to augment those under the platforms of the transit sheds. As many as 120 horses were provided for, their boxes partly ventilated by openings on the canal side of the arches.[14] Flanking the approach to the viaduct, offices were built to serve that end of the yard, particularly the coal trade, and they gradually acquired a jagged profile when they were sporadically extended at various heights in the late 1850s.

The road past the offices led to the coal and stone docks, all with their own rail connections, and beyond them to the engine sheds. No other part of the yard as seen today hides its past so well, for the sheds were demolished at the end of the steam age in 1963 and now even the most assiduous archaeologist will have difficulty in identifying exactly where they stood. Their disappearance, before a proper record of them had been made, has erased one part of the King's Cross story which deserved a better fate. Photographs show that the principal shed, built in 1850 on a fan-shaped plan and providing twenty-five arched entrances to the engine roads, survived to the very end.[15] It would have been interesting to know whether the wrought iron trussed roof that it originally had – one of the kind common to buildings across the site – lasted as long as the rest of the building.

When the engineer William Humber gave a lecture on railway buildings and layouts in 1865 he applauded the design of the King's Cross Goods Yard: 'the whole is conveniently arranged, and the site is well chosen'.[16] That was praise indeed for a project which had been carried out at considerable speed in slightly anxious circumstances, and was completed before the Great Northern had a clear idea of the traffic it would have to handle. The foresight that Cubitt showed in providing buildings large and flexible enough to meet most eventualities had proved amply correct. Had he been less successful fewer of his buildings would be available for us to admire well over a century later. Yet there were many changes that, even with the best advice available, he could not have predicted would happen. These too have to be accounted for in understanding the appearance of the goods yard today.

One of these changes was referred to by Humber, but without his acknowledging that it had involved an alteration to the original layout. Soon after the yard opened it began to win some of the London potato trade away from its traditional centre at Tooley Street in Southwark. Whether or not the Great Northern actively courted such trade is unclear, but its yard was certainly more convenient for Covent Garden and, unlike the sea carriers on whom Tooley Street depended, it could offer a regular supply regardless of the weather. But waggon-loads of potatoes used up considerable space, almost as much as coal, and it was embarrassing that no special accommodation had been allowed for them in the original plan. It was therefore a blessing that, contrary to William Cubitt's forebodings, the temporary passenger station proved true to its name and closed when the main line station opened in 1852. Soon afterwards its buildings and roofs were adapted and extended for use by the potato trade, for which they seemed more than adequate.[17] However, within a decade that

generous measure had to be reconsidered. By then the trade had reached 85,000 tons a year, jamming the yard and causing problems of storage; and the merchants, who seemed to have been less well cared for than their commodity, were complaining about the wooden huts, 'not unlike sentry-boxes', which served as their offices. This time the Great Northern was forced to build afresh by adding a series of thirty-nine small warehouses, strung out between the old station and Maiden Lane. Each of these had its own siding, capable of holding up to four waggons, plus cellar space for storage. The sidings were reached by an elaborate series of turntables on the lines in the old station.[18]

The area which today is referred to as the potato market comprises the 1864–5 warehouses, plus a roof added over their roadway in 1896–7, but since these structures have been either demolished or removed their title is a matter of history. However there is one further section built for the potato trade which still survives, though like the rest of the yard it is without the tracks which once gave it life. In 1888 the merchants pointed out to the Great Northern the superior facilities for potato handling that the Midland Railway was providing at its depot in Somers Town. The Midland, they argued, had put them at a disadvantage, particularly because some of the area that they were forced to use – between the old passenger station and the Midland Shed – was exposed to the elements. Richard Johnson, the Great Northern engineer, responded by devising a set of roofs to encase the Midland Shed on three sides. As the maker's plates on their columns announcee these roofs were fabricated by

59. (Opposite) The original crescent-shaped engine shed, roofed by Cubitt trusses similar to those over the temporary terminus.

60. (Opposite) The goods yard offices.

61. (Above) King's Cross engine shed in the last days of steam. None of these buildings now survives.

62. *The potato market in 1864, just before the building of more permanent warehouses.*

Andrew Handyside and Co., whose tender of £14,835 came in well below Johnson's estimate.[19] The larger of the Handyside roofs, between the Midland Shed and the wall of the eastern transit shed, consists of a series of Warren truss girders supporting transverse roofs with wrought iron trusses. On the other side of the shed, where the span covered is less, the trusses form a continuous curved gable; their line of support on the outer side incorporates the spandrel beams from the old passenger station already referred to.

The potato trade at King's Cross seems to have reached a peak after the First World War. In 1921 124,000 tons of produce were dealt with, including not just potatoes but other staple vegetables such as turnips, peas, celery and cabbage. Fish was the other main perishable, most of it sent on to Billingsgate but retained for sale at King's Cross on Sundays when that market was closed.[20] Long after the smell has departed railwaymen still remember the area under the larger Handyside roofs as the 'Long and Short Fish Road'.

Potatoes and coal were the principal commodities that were dealt with in such quantities that special buildings had to be provided for them. Most of the other goods passing through King's Cross made no separate claims to attention but were dealt with collectively in the Granary and the transit sheds. Ample though these buildings once seemed, by the 1890s they were choked with traffic; that was, after all, a time when almost all long-distance goods went by rail. So in 1897 it was decided to build a new warehouse over the coal and stone basin, and to turn the neighbouring western coal drops into a goods shed. Together these would handle the outward goods, leaving the transit sheds and Granary exclusively for the inward goods. The new warehouse, completed in 1899, was a two-level affair: with tracks going in on both floors it could take 150 waggons at a time. Alexander Ross, the engineer who designed it, set his sights no higher than utility demanded; as a result that shed has never attracted much attention as part of the whole goods yard group except, that is, for the goods platform in the old western coal drop, which kept its original roof and gained an attractive canopy over the adjoining road.[21]

More traffic also meant more paperwork. The new goods shed had offices above its first floor level for some of the staff needed for checking and recording the invoices which poured through every day. The old transit shed area, although it already had offices attached, needed more space to match. This was provided by the erection of a single storey block above part of the train assembly area, to be reached by a corridor running off the Granary. Alexander Ross again went for a straightfoward solution, which in this case meant using part of the old 1850 transit shed roof at the new level.[22] The effect of his resourcefulness has been that, although the offices have long since gone out of use, it is possible to see running above them a well-preserved example of the standard type of roof that Cubitt used.

Apart from new and adapted buildings, the other main way that the yard had altered by the end of the century was that it had been broken up by viaducts. The two sets of coal drops appear always to have had adjacent viaducts for removing the empty waggons, but these did not interfere with the roads in the yard. The two viaducts that were added later both crossed the Regent's Canal and so were far more obtrusive. The first of these – originally of timber but rebuilt in engineering brick – cut its way between the two coal drops to a bridge over the canal leading to Samuel Plimsoll's coal drops. The bridge has now gone, leaving the viaduct bereft of purpose. The other, which has entirely disappeared, went along one side of the granary basin to a bridge which fed directly into the retort houses of the gas works.

The presence of these viaducts, and of railway tracks going into most of the goods yard buildings, might suggest at first glance that the yard was alive with shunting engines moving waggons and assembling trains. Quite the reverse was true. Because of the danger of fire, and because it was dangerous and cumbersome to use an engine to move one or two waggons, engines were conspicuously absent from the innermost parts of the yard. Instead three other kinds of traction were relied on – human muscle, horses and hydraulic power. Of these three, evidence for only the second two remains, for ironically the labour force that ran the yard, without which nothing would have moved, demanded least in the way of special accommodation. Most of its fuelling and welfare was looked after in homes far beyond the boundaries of the site.

Horses were used for moving waggons but had a much more important role as fetchers and carriers linking the yard to the outside world. It was clearly because of such uses that stabling for as many as 500 horses was thought necessary in 1851. As already mentioned, the first stabling was provided beneath the transit shed platforms, a dark and cramped location which not surprisingly was later condemned as 'altogether unfitted' for its purpose'.[23] The stables beneath the roadway viaduct, completed at about the same time, at least had the benefit of open air and daylight. Nine years after the yard had opened 800 horses worked there, and by the turn of the century it was claimed that the Great Northern employed 1,500 horses on deliveries.[24] Such figures were proof – if ever it were needed – that the railways, far from being the enemy of the horse, had multiplied the demand for horse-labour dramatically. It seems inconceivable that all of the Great Northern's horses were kept at King's Cross overnight, but undoubtedly there were other stables tucked in odd corners of the yard that absorbed a high proportion of them.

Whereas the railway's use of horses perpetuated traditional working methods, the choice of hydraulic power for the goods yard was an innovative, if not rather daring decision. Hydraulic engineering was developed by William Armstrong (later Lord Armstrong) in the later 1840s, principally as a way of powering cranes. His main achievement was to overcome the need for a huge reservoir to maintain hydraulic pressure by substituting an accumulator. This used a weighted ram to achieve the same effect, providing power in a more compact and flexible way. In 1851, when the Great Northern directors had to

63. The curved Handyside roof alongside Midland Shed.

choose what kind of mechanical power to install in the Granary and transit sheds, reliable hydraulic machinery had only recently become available (one of Armstrong's first customers was Jesse Hartley, engineer of the Albert Dock in Liverpool). So it was courageous of them to select Armstrong's equipment though, after a slight hiccup over his delivery date, their confidence in him proved well-founded.[25]

Nothing remains of the hydraulic engine house, which was built between the eastern coal drops and the granary basin. From there power was piped to the Granary hoists, worked by hydraulic jiggers and to the capstans used throughout the site for moving waggons. Some of the capstans can still be seen, for instance, one on the eastern coal drop viaduct and another in the Midland Shed. But far more interesting than these is the survival of a subsidiary accumulator at the north end of the Midland Shed. Installed later than the original equipment, it was presumably intended to boost the power supply to the potato market sidings after they had been extended in 1864–5. The accumulator tank fits snugly into a brick-built tower, constrained by guide rails fitted to

64. The western goods shed seen from across the Midland main line, with the Granary in the distance.

65. The hydraulic pumping station in front of the Granary, photographed in 1979 (since demolished).

HYDRAULIC ACCUMULATOR, MIDLAND SHED
(Not to scale)

A   Guide rail

B   Ballast (iron and gravel)

C   Piston

D   Pressurising cylinder

E   Hydraulic main

F   Ballast tank (iron plates)

G   Timber buffing block

H   Timber frame

J   Iron stay

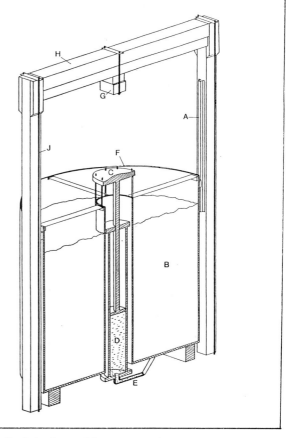

66. The hydraulic accumulator, Midland shed.

massive timbers in the walls. It had no additional pumping engine, but must have relied instead on the main 1851 engine or, just possibly, on a hydraulic main supplying power from outside the site. Although it was installed as an afterthought, now that most of the hydraulic system has disappeared this accumulator stands as the single most interesting piece of equipment in the yard.

For the whole of its working life in this century the goods yard has lived off its nineteenth-century inheritance of buildings and facilities. Some modest additions have been made – a locomotive coaling plant in 1931, and more recently the equipment for handling Freightliner containers: as the last to come, these have been amongst the first to go. Until goods trains finally ceased running from the yard they were dealt with much as they always had been; electric lifts were introduced, lorries replaced horse-drawn carts, but the process of loading and unloading trains changed little from the time the yard first opened.

It would not be hard to portray this perpetuation of traditional methods as symptomatic of Britain's industrial failure. Yet, as with the other stalwart industries of the nineteenth century, there is equally a case to be argued that, even if the yard had been totally rebuilt and re-equipped, it would still have been overtaken by events. Once lorries had proved their worth in long-distance goods haulage railways were bound to lose a fair proportion of that traffic, even with the best goods yards available. In 1938 there were thirty-eight goods trains coming into the yard every day, and thirty trains out.[26] Today there is just an occasional train supplying the concrete batching plant at the north end of the site. To rub home this change of fortune, the warehouses which are still used for goods are supplied by the busy lorries of the National Freight Corporation.

Whether it would have been worthwhile for the railways to re-equip the goods yard is a matter still open to debate though, in view of what has happened, it must seem a rather academic question. If modernisation had taken place it might have saved the railway freight traffic for a few more years, but with one grievous side-effect. Many of the buildings on the site which are now so admired would no doubt have been replaced, or simply swept away to save the cost of their upkeep. As it is, by the process of benign neglect they have been kept, and so they stand a good chance of starting a new post-railway existence in which they will be appreciated as much as ever.

FOOTNOTES

1 Malcolm Tucker, 'Bricklayers' Arms Station', *London's Industrial Archaeology*, 4, (1989), 1–23.
2 Charles Dickens, *Our Mutual Friend*, (Penguin edn. 1971), 76. Although written in 1863–5 some of the material in the novel draws on Dickens's earlier experiences. The symbolic importance of the dust-heaps has often been discussed by literary scholars, e.g. Harvey Sucksmith, 'The Dust Heaps in *Our Mutual Friend*', *Essays in Criticism* XXIII (April 1973), 206–12.
3 John R. Kellett, *The Impact of Railways on Victorian Cities*, (1969), 272; Select Committee on Railway and Canal Legislation, *Parliamentary Papers* 1857–8, XIV, 127.
4 Public Record Office, RAIL 236/273: Letters of 31 May 1849 (William Cubitt), 27 Sept 1849 (William and Joseph Cubitt) and 6 Dec 1849 (Joseph Cubitt).
5 RAIL 236/15: GNR Board 6 Dec 1849; RAIL 236/239: GNR Station Committee 14 Jan 1850.
6 RAIL 236/273: Letters of 17 July 1850 (Joseph Cubitt) and 7 April 1851 (Joseph Cubitt); John Wrottesley, *The Great Northern Railway*, 1, (1979), 53–5.
7 RAIL 236/239: GNR Station Committee, 14 Jan 1850.
8 H.R. Johnson and A.W. Skempton, 'William Strutt's Cotton Mills, 1793–1812', *Transactions of the Newcomen Society* XXX (1955–7), 179–205; Ron Fitzgerald, 'The Development of the Cast Iron Frame in Textile Mills to 1850', *Industrial Archaeology Review*, X, (Spring 1988), 127–45.
9 RAIL 236/273: Letter of 7 Feb 1851 (Joseph Cubitt).
10 Drawings and Specification for GNR London Terminus Iron Roofs, March 1850 (Institution of Civil Engineers Library);

see also Thomas Tredgold, *Elementary Principles of Carpentry*, (5th edn. 1870), plate 50.
11 RAIL 236/239: GNR Station Committee, 14 Jan 1850.
12 Drawings and Specification, op.cit.; *Observer*, 27 April 1851, 7.
13 Drawings and Specification, op.cit.; *Illustrated London News*, 30 Aug 1851, 265.
14 RAIL 236/72: GNR Executive Committee, 19 Mar 1851.
15 P.N. Townend, *Top Shed* (1975), 9–13.
16 William Humber, 'On the Design and arrangement of Railway Stations, Repairing Shops, Engine sheds etc', *Minutes of the Proceedings of the Institution of Civil Engineers*, XXV (1865–66).
17 RAIL 236/276/2: Reports of Joseph Cubitt 1853.
18 *Illustrated Times*, 1 Oct 1864, 210; 'King's Cross Potato Market, LNER', *LNER Magazine* XXIX (March 1929), 134–6.
19 RAIL 236/362/18: Covering over Potato Market, King's Cross, 1888.
20 Cuthbert Maughan, *Markets of London* (1931), 173–5; W.J. Passingham, *London Markets* (1934), 115–19.
21 RAIL 236/532: Contract and Specification, 6 Dec 1897; *Transport*, 7 Jul 1899, 26–27.
22 RAIL 236/530: Contract and Specification, 4 Feb 1898.
23 RAIL 236/367/8: Professor J. Wortley Axe's Report on GNR Horse Stock, 1891.
24 Unattributed cutting, 10 Sep 1859, Heal Collection, Swiss Cottage Library; J. Medcalf, 'King's Cross Goods Station', *Railway Magazine* IV (April 1900), 319.
25 RAIL 236/71: GNR Executive Committee, 29 Jan 1851; RAIL 236/16: GNR Board, 5 Aug 1851.
26 G.A. Roberts, 'Remodelling of King's Cross Goods Station', *LNER Magazine* XXVIII (Nov 1938), 635.

67. *Coal bound for London.*

68. *The coal drops c1895.*
Plimsoll's drops, served by the
Great Northern, faced Midland
Railway drops on the opposite side
of Cambridge (later Camley)
Street.

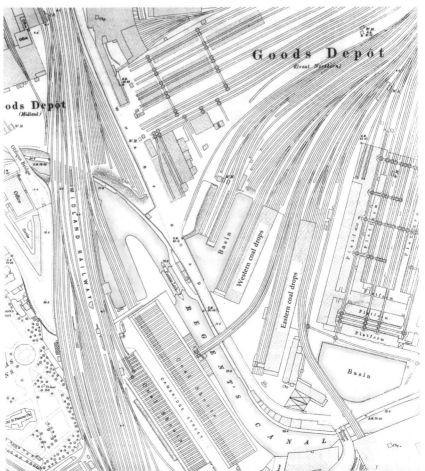

CHAPTER SIX

The Great Northern Railway and the London Coal Trade

Robert Thorne

From the outset railways were intimately linked to the coal trade, first as pithead waggonways then in the form of fully-fledged lines connecting collieries to local towns or ports. The Stockton and Darlington Railway, usually venerated as the principal forbear of the British railway system, was developed to link the Durham coalfield to the River Tees. From its example sprang the Leicester and Swannington Railway, built to improve the supply of coal to Leicester, followed a few years later by the most famous coal line of all – the Taff Vale Railway, running inland from Cardiff to the coalfields around Merthyr and up the Rhondda Valley. But all of these were local lines and so they did not directly exploit the biggest prize of all, the supply of domestic and industrial coal to the metropolis.

Before the railway revolution, London's immense appetite for coal had been satisfied by sea-borne coal from the northeast coalfields. This trade was fundamental to London's dominant position in the English economy and to the development of London industries. Such was the procession of colliers down the east coast that often the amount of coal supplied from the north-east ports was more than the total volume of national imports. By the end of the 1820s the quantity of coal being brought up the Thames each year exceeded two million tons, and it had reached over three million tons by the late 1840s.[1] It is hardly surprising that the railways sought to gain a share of this traffic, not just in the supporting role of transporting coal to the ports but by taking it the whole distance to London. As carriers they could offer a regular supply, unaffected by wind or weather, and their waggonloads, brought to purpose-built railheads, were more convenient for domestic distribution than bulk loads brought by collier. Above all, railways were ideally suited to serving coalfields far from the sea, such as those of South Yorkshire and the East Midlands. By creating new routes for coal to London they were in a position to transform the geography of coal supply.

By the time the railways set out to rival it, the sea-borne trade had achieved a number of improvements within its long-established practice. Sailing colliers were owned by consortia, which often included mine owners. The ship's master bought the load on behalf of the owners, and sold it at the end of the trip through the medium of a London factor. By the early nineteenth century a collier was expected to be able to make ten round trips a year between the north-east and London, carrying 260–300 tons. This represented an improvement in timing and tonnage compared with a hundred years earlier, but it was hard to see how any further gains in productivity could be squeezed from the existing system. More trips were being made than previously mainly because steam tugs had been introduced to haul colliers out to sea when there was an adverse wind, and to assist them in getting up the Thames. More efficient loading staithes had accelerated the taking on of coal. But a fundamental obstacle to greater efficiency occurred when ships arrived at their destination, for unloading into a lighter could occupy six days or more, to be followed by a further delay while taking on ballast for the return voyage. There was also a limit on the number of colliers allowed into the Pool of London at any one time.[2]

The most obvious sign that the sea-borne trade was being stretched to its limit was the harrowing tally of losses along the coast. Sailing forth with six hands or less on board, and perhaps over-loaded, a collier was particularly vulnerable to the perils of bad weather in the North Sea. It was a fortunate ship that survived its expected lifespan of thirty years without mishap for, as the Royal National Lifeboat Institution reported in 1867, half the losses in British waters were of 'unseaworthy, overloaded and ill-found vessels of the collier class.'[3] Most of the wrecks were of ships making their way south from the Tyne and Tees, on the main coal route.

The railways never seem to have exploited the comparison between safety on land and sea in the battle over the coal trade, presumably because coal merchants were more interested in the price on delivery than the human cost of bringing the commodity to London. But even if accusations about the safety of colliers were not voiced directly by the railways, the problem was brought to public attention, and held there vociferously, by a coal merchant whose interests were closely tied to rail transport. As will subsequently emerge, that same merchant played a significant part in the development of coal-handling at King's Cross, so there is an intriguing link via his career between this somewhat specialised study and the wider public issues of the period.

The first supply of coal to London by rail was made in 1845, when the London and Birmingham Railway brought consignments from Derbyshire via Rugby. That year the railway contribution to the overall supply of the metropolis was a paltry 8,377 tons, but in the following years it multiplied so fast that by 1856 railways were responsible for 28.5% of the London trade.[4] The company which did more than any other to break the sea carriers' monopoly was the Great Northern. Through links with the North Eastern Railway it invaded the north-east, while simultaneously opening up new sources in the coal producing areas of South Yorkshire. The intention of making the line to King's Cross an artery of the coal trade was in the company's mind from the beginning, and the planning of the goods yard (more fully discussed in Chapter Five) gave as much priority to that trade as to any of its other functions. As *Herapath's Journal* expressed it in 1854.'It may be said that *the* traffic of the Great Northern Railway is coal'.[5]

The most conspicuous facility for handling the coal traffic in the goods yard was the long set of coal drops immediately to the west of the Granary, approached by rail at the same level as the other buildings and by road at a lower level. When brought into use in 1851, it was predicted that these would be capable of handling a thousand tons a day.[6] Beyond them was the second of the two canal basins in the yard, created partly for the transfer of coal from railway to canal. It was often said that the railways would obliterate canal traffic as decisively as they had driven stage coaches from the roads but in instances such as this, when the effort was made to secure a link between the two, there were benefits to be gained on both sides. In 1856 almost 200,000 tons of coal was transferred onwards by canal from King's Cross, presumably mostly to industries which had developed on canalside sites.[7] Three years later so much

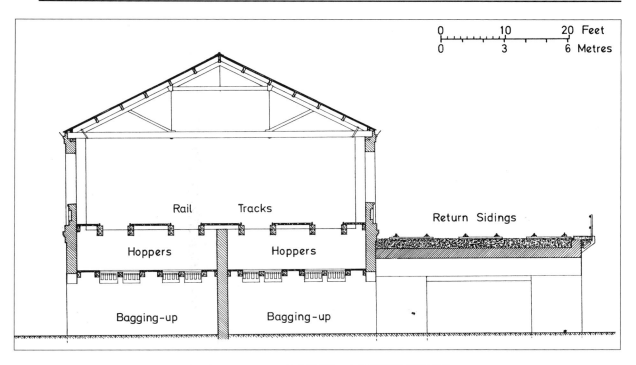

Rail   Tracks

Return Sidings

Hoppers   Hoppers

Bagging-up   Bagging-up

*69. Section through the eastern
coal drops and its adjacent viaduct.*

*70. Loading bay openings in the
eastern coal drops.*

*71. The eastern coal drops,
photographed not long before the
fire of 1985.*

coal was being brought from the Midlands and the North that the Great Northern decided to build a second set of drops alongside the coal trade basin. Finished in 1860, and known as the western coal drops to distinguish them from their predecessor, these have survived in an altered state long after the basin has gone.[8]

The two coal drop buildings present the most tantalising historical problems on the whole goods yard site. The axiom that once something is out of use it is soon forgotten is vividly illustrated in the difficulties of reconstructing how exactly they functioned in their heyday. From the way they hold their secrets they could as well be survivors of the Roman occupation as structures only recently abandoned. Essentially there are two obstacles to understanding their original use. First, as is so often the case with industrial buildings, their operation was so taken for granted that it never occurred to anyone to record it. Oddly enough, the only printed description of them dates from 1851 and was written on the basis of advance information before they were completed. Secondly, the evidence that they present today is partial and confusing because one set was converted to another use at the turn of the century and the other was badly damaged by fire in 1985. It is galling to think how many simple problems of interpretation would have been solved if someone had shown the foresight to record the drops even a decade ago.

Despite their fire-gutted northern end, the eastern coal drops are the easier of the two structures to understand, most of all because it is possible to see their full length and height on the Granary side. What are missing are the railway tracks which once served them, and all but fragments of their coal handling apparatus. Four tracks came in on the upper level, where they were carried on longitudinal timber baulks. The structure below was divided into forty-eight cells, arranged on either side of a spine wall. Each cell housed a coal drop mechanism consisting of a hopper at mezzanine level just below the tracks and two cart-loading bays at ground level. It was the system for releasing coal from

72. The western coal drops as converted to warehouse use.

the hoppers which most impressed the writer of 1851 who reported on the yet incomplete structure.'In the floor of the stores', he said, 'are a series of shoots, six to each bay, through which the coals can either be discharged in bulk, or their flow can be regulated so as to allow of their easily being put in sacks.'[9] Today only a few fragments of the chutes survive, along with the claws which regulated the discharge of coal. There is no clear sign how they were operated.

Great Northern coal waggons, of 7½ tons capacity, had bottom openings so that they could discharge directly into the coal drop hoppers.[10] Having been emptied they were hauled to the southern end of the drops where, with the aid of a traverser, they were moved sideways onto a viaduct on the west side of the building. The viaduct that survives today is not quite as long as the original one so it is hard to appreciate exactly how it used to function. As shown on early maps of the site, it stretched beyond the traverser so that brake vans could be stored at its dead end ready to be used on return trains of empty waggons. This ingenious layout enabled coal trains to be turned round quite efficiently, though it had no flexibility to allow for the use of larger waggons.

Nowadays, when so much of the apparatus of the eastern coal drops has disappeared, it is the structure of the building which attracts most attention: its handsome brick arcading, its ironwork and its roof. In common with the other buildings of the Lewis Cubitt era the brickwork is plain and straightforward, except for the panelled parapets of the upper level openings and curious circular features, which must have served some purpose, in the external wall of the mezzanine hopper floor. Within an essentially brick structure, iron plays a subsidiary and slightly deceptive role. At ground level every alternate support in the loading bay openings is provided by a cast iron column with a diamond-shaped feature above the capital. At a casual glance it appears that this feature is a solid casting, providing the springing for the brickwork arches above, but in fact it is a decorative plate cast as part of the beam which carries the loading bay ceiling. The siting of the columns is also slightly illogical, for they are placed flush with the face of the building rather than beneath the centre of the wall they support. Looking into the openings it is a relief to see that the ceiling beam is supported by a second column playing a more obvious structural role. The ceiling timbers which span from the beam to the wall of each cell once carried the hoppers and chute apparatus. No doubt if, as is hoped, at least part of this building is restored to its original form, it will be possible for a visitor to work out how each element in it functioned; but before that stage is reached there will still be a number of archaeological puzzles to be solved.

At the end of the last century the southern end of the eastern coal drops was converted into a warehouse, but the brick infill left most of the ironwork intact. The original roof was also left untouched, with the result that it can still be seen today above the offices and studios which now occupy the warehouse. The roof at the other end was totally destroyed in the fire of a few years ago. Compared with the trusses in the roofs over the temporary passenger station and the goods shed, those which support the coal drop roof seem slightly less innovative. Most of the main parts are timber – the tie beams, rafters, collars and struts – leaving wrought iron to provide the queen post rods, other rods connecting the collar to the apex of the roof, and the plates which secure the rafters to the tie beams. But if this roof is recreated above the burnt-out section it will undoubtedly prove an impressive sight.

Though finished slightly later, it appears that the western coal drops embodied essentially the same system as their predecessor. Again there were four tracks running over a series of cells, thirty in all, with an adjacent viaduct for handling the empty waggons. Presumably there was also some kind of mezzanine floor containing the coal hoppers but this, along with the rest of the coal handling equipment, was removed when the building was converted into a goods shed in 1897–99: the traverser at the southern end was also taken out. The main features of the 1890s shed, as can still be seen today, were a raised platform with a timber curb and a new roadway alongside carried on massive cast iron columns. The conundrum in this arrangement is that the new platform does not fill the whole of the shed, there being a single rail track at a slightly lower level along its west side. The specification for the conversion

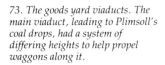

73. *The goods yard viaducts. The main viaduct, leading to Plimsoll's coal drops, had a system of differing heights to help propel waggons along it.*

works suggests that the platform was erected at a new level, but was carried on the same system of longitudinal iron beams as the original coal drop tracks: the engineer conscientiously insisted that even the padstones from the older structure should be incorporated in the new arrangement.[11]

Throughout the course of these complicated alterations the roof over the western coal drops was left largely unscathed. Spanning the full 48ft. width of the building, it has composite trusses of a slightly more complex kind than those over the earlier set of drops. The rafters and collar of each truss are timber, as is the upright from collar to apex. The queen posts and tie-bars are wrought iron, and the two diagonal struts are cast iron. There are plenty of mid-Victorian roofs which achieve more spectacular effects, but as a characteristic example of a straightforward solution this cannot be bettered.

It is easy to become so preoccupied with the coal drops as industrial monuments that their essential purpose is lost sight of. They were, after all, simply a staging-post in the process by which coal got from the coalmines to the consumer, and the way that overall procedure was organised was as important as the technology employed. In this respect what was important about the Great Northern, apart from the vigour it put into the business, was that it chose not just to carry coal but to market it as well. It seemed logical as well as profitable to do so, and it could be claimed that it brought advantage to the consumer by eliminating at least one tier of middle men. The first coal manager the company appointed was Coles Child, already well-known in the trade. In 1854 he was succeeded by Herbert Clarke, brother of the general manager. But if the system seemed to work well from the company's point of view it appeared highly objectionable to the London coal merchants, and to some coal owners: in their eyes, the cordial relationship between the coal manager and the rest of the railway's management did nothing to make things better.

The way the Great Northern handled the trade did not exclude independent coal merchants from obtaining supplies over its line, but those that tried to do so found that the rates they were charged made it hard for them to compete with the company's own agent, or that their initiatives were frustrated in other ways. The coal owners' main grievance was that the trade was being restricted in favour of a limited number of firms. They also complained that Herbert Clarke was unfitted for his post, as was manifest in the way he allowed coal from different collieries to become mixed up together. That might not matter to some customers, but with firms such as gas companies, which had been persuaded to take a particular type of coal for its burning qualities, it meant a loss of trade.[12]

But as always the crucial argument was a legal one. The Act of 1846 which established the Great Northern, like all other railway acts, sanctioned its powers on the understanding that it would act as a public carrier. It nowhere mentioned a right to trade in coal. In 1860 a case against the company was brought in the Court of Chancery at the instigation of Thomas North, a Nottinghamshire coal owner. It was established that over the years the Great Northern had purchased far more coal than it could possibly need for its own use: 800,000 tons in 1856, and only slightly less the following year. Vice-Chancellor Kindersley was staggered to find that, by 'a most crafty and tricky contrivance', the profits from its coal trade had been concealed in the general traffic account. It was obvious what had been going on, and equally it seemed indisputable that the company had acted in restraint of trade. The Court decreed that it should give up the business and throw open the trade.[13]

The effect of this judgement on the goods yard was the arrival of a dozen or more coal merchants and coal owners as tenants of the facilities which until then had been operated exclusively by the company. Merchants such as Rickett and Smith hung up their boards in the coal offices and many of the coal drops were occupied by coal owners, including Messrs. Newton Chambers and Co.

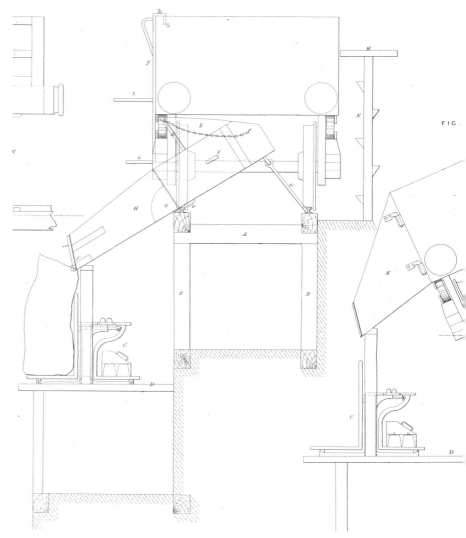

FIG.

74. *Samuel Plimsoll (1824–98),*
from a watercolour by W. Vine,
published in Vanity Fair, *1873.*

75. *Part of Plimsoll's 1859 Patent,*
showing a hopper raised beneath a
bottom-opening waggon.

and the Silkstone Collieries of South Yorkshire. Herbert Clarke, the victim of so much previous odium, stayed on as an independent merchant.[14]

The names of those who moved into the coal offices are probably meaningless to all but specialist historians, with one exception. Samuel Plimsoll, later famous for his boisterous, inept, but ultimately successful campaign for the safety of merchant shipping, had been one of the most vehement objectors to the monopoly exercised by the Great Northern. Having worked in a solicitor's office in Sheffield, and as a clerk in a brewery, he entered the coal business in 1853. Frustrated by the refusal of the company to handle his waggons between Barnsley and London, he advocated the advantages of an unrestricted trade at a shareholders' meeting in 1854. Whatever sympathy he might have attracted was counteracted by the revelation that he had lied about his status as a proprietor in order to gain access to the meeting.[15] Taking advantage of this disqualification the company continued to allow his waggons to stand empty

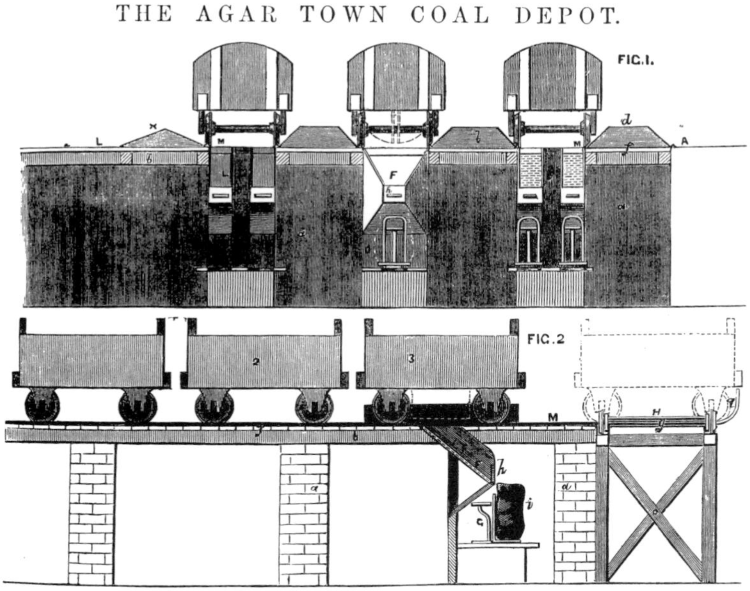

THE AGAR TOWN COAL DEPOT.

FIG.1.

FIG.2.

76. Cross-section through Plimsoll's coal drops, as illustrated in Engineering *for 1867.*

and unused, and he was declared bankrupt the following year.[16] However, within a year he had returned to London to pursue his case: as shipowners were later to discover, setbacks only seemed to increase his determination. The Great Northern agreed to deliver coal for him to King's Cross, to be transferred to the canal, at the rate of 250 tons a week.[17] With the support of the Yorkshire coal owners, one of whose step-daughters he married, he convinced London gas companies to use him as their agent. In 1858 one such company contracted to take 52,000 tons of Yorkshire coal supplied by him.[18] With an eye to yet wider markets he took on the mantle of Thomas Cook by organising a day trip to the coalfields for London merchants. The fact that about 195 people took tickets for his special train was a sign, if one were still needed, that he was spearheading a more ruthlessly competitive phase in the development of the trade.[19]

It looked as if Plimsoll was getting what he wanted, even before the Chancery decision of 1860. But in one further respect he was still dissatisfied with the service that the Great Northern provided. The coal drops, ingenious though they were, seemed to him to have a fundamental deficiency. Even when the hoppers were full, waggons discharging into them dropped the coal from quite a height, smashing it in a clatter of noise and dust. In a busy year the financial loss from such breakages was bound to be considerable. Plimsoll therefore decided to devise an alternative system, which he patented in 1859. This allowed the coal to be discharged in two different ways: either by tilting the whole waggon in order to shoot it into the waiting sacks, or by raising a hopper against the underside of the waggon down which it could flow into sacks alongside.[20] Of these two methods, Plimsoll eventually opted for the second, in a more developed form which allowed the sacks to be put directly under the hopper in a pit beneath the tracks. Except that the coal did not have so far to fall, this was not so very different to the apparatus of the existing drops. The alternative idea of jacking up one side of the waggon must have presented an alarming risk of turning the whole thing over – wrecking the container to get at its contents.

A month after registering his patent Plimsoll applied to the Great Northern for space in the goods yard to construct a prototype version. It was a sign of the way the company's attitude was turning that this project was permitted well before the Chancery case was heard, though the directors protected their interests by insisting that he took 40,000 tons of coal a year for unloading. His experimental drops were inexpensive and short-lived. No remains of them can now be seen, but evidently they were provocatively sited alongside the two Great Northern coal drops which Plimsoll so despised.[21]

Satisfied by the success of his experiment, Plimsoll wanted more space for his operations, so the boundaries of the goods yard had to be expanded for the first time since it was first laid out. By 1865, the year that his ambitions came to a head, the yard was already well hemmed in, but there was a cluster of houses, stables and canalside wharves on the far side of the canal in what appeared to be an ideal spot. The Great Northern had no difficulty in clearing these properties, and in a joint project with Plimsoll built a viaduct (mostly of timber, but incorporating an iron bridge) across the canal to reach the new site.[22] This was no ordinary viaduct, for it was designed in two halves to give the benefit of gravity to horses pulling waggons along it. Going towards Plimsoll's new drops one half sloped gradually down from a raised hump in the yard, while the other half used a slope in the other direction to help empty trucks on their way. The drops themselves were built in a rank alongside the canal where today the Camley Street Natural Park flourishes. They relied on two traversers, at the front and back of the structure, to circulate the waggons, ensuring that empty waggons never jammed the positions that full ones required. The traversers, powered at first by horse but later by steam, were also contrived to make use of gravity as much as possible.

As opened in 1866, Plimsoll's drops had thirteen sidings, all fitted with his approved kind of coal-conserving hoppers. In the first week of operation they handled 1,575 tons. During the following year they got into their stride sufficiently to handle about a sixth of the tonnage passing through the yard.[23] Though no trace of them survives, they have the advantage over the other drops that they were fully reported on when new: another example of Plimsoll's shrewd eye for publicity.[24] Whether they were imitated elsewhere is a question that remains to be answered.

Many characteristics of Plimsoll's career as a coal merchant can be seen as a foretaste of his more celebrated role as saviour of the merchant seamen – his energy, his tenacity and his occasional unscrupulousness. He was already on the way to achieving his reputation for being, in Disraeli's words, 'half rogue and half enthusiast'.[25] Biographers have willingly entered into the game of spotting the common strands in his behaviour, but none of them appear to have been alert to a possible connection between his business interests and his campaigning fervour. In a more cynical age than his, one of the first questions to be asked would be whether his attack on negligent shipowners was not at least partly motivated by a desire to curb his rivals in the London·coal trade. The charts in his best-selling book *Our Seamen* (1873) confirmed, as was already well-known, that a high proportion of the wrecks around Britain were in the sea lanes down the east coast used by colliers. To improve the safety of such ships by restricting loads and imposing minimum standards of seaworthiness was bound to have implications for the competitiveness of the sea-borne trade. Bearing that in mind, it is difficult to believe that Plimsoll's battle on behalf of the seamen was wholly altruistic. Yet apparently no-one at the time suspected his motives, not even the shipowners whom he berated for their iniquities. And from his point of view in 1870, when he first took up the cudgels on behalf of the seamen, his business had little to fear from competition. In fact he was able to leave much of its management to others, to accept a seat in Parliament, and to cast around for a cause to call his own. His merchant shipping campaign

bore a tangential relation to a world he already knew well, but if there was any trace of conspiracy in his conduct it did not arouse the suspicion of his contemporaries.

Having described the opening of his Camley Street drops, most biographers of Plimsoll quite rightly turn their attention to his political activities. But while he took to the campaign trail the goods yard that helped supply his income underwent further transformation – not so much in its appearance and equipment as in its prominence in the coal trade. The expansion of London's suburbs made it increasingly inefficient to supply every outreach of the metropolis from a central depot. Recognising the value of the suburban trade, the Great Northern not only opened subsidiary depots on its own lines, but in a more venturesome manner exploited the connection it had with south London via Farringdon and Blackfriars to develop a coal business far from its usual territory. In this respect Plimsoll does not fade from the story, for he helped colonise the new areas by opening a depot at Elephant and Castle. By the end of the century a significant proportion of the coal brought into London by the Great Northern was diverted to other destinations before it reached King's Cross. The Ferme Park yard, opened between Hornsey and Harringey in 1888, became the great sorting-point for through traffic.

Suburban outposts were a logical development in the coal trade, but they were also a way of resisting competition. As leaders in the development of the rail-borne coal trade the Great Northern could hardly expect to have a high proportion of the field to itself indefinitely, yet it was particularly tormenting that its principal rival came to the fore with its assistance. When the Midland Railway began to run trains to King's Cross in 1858, part of the agreement allowed it to use facilities in the goods yard (including the ex-carriage shed already discussed in Chapter Five) and at Holloway. The Midland was as closely associated with the coalfields of the East Midlands as the Great Northern was with South Yorkshire, and despite the tolls exacted by the Great Northern, coal supplied from Midland territory was soon a familiar sight in London. Indeed the Midland traffic became so large that in 1862 special sidings were built at King's Cross to handle it.[26]

The main advantage that the Midland had was simply that its coalfields were closer to London. Hoping to join in that good fortune, the Great Northern decided in 1862 to build its own line into the East Midlands coalfield, linked to its line from Nottingham to Grantham. Rather than accept this intrusion the Midland negotiated an agreement allowing the Great Northern to have access to coal in its area in return for the withdrawal of the minimum toll exacted on its coal trains using King's Cross. That may have seemed quite equitable, but a further aspect of the same agreement precipitated a conflict between the two companies which dragged on for a decade. At the insistence of the Midland the Great Northern accepted that there should be a permanent differential in tonnage rates in favour of Midlands coal against South Yorkshire coal.

A hundred or more years later, a conflict over railway freight rates can easily seem as arcane as a squabble between protestant sects, but since the subject was of immediate importance to the fuel supply of London it is hardly surprising that the press eagerly reported every bout. The 1863 agreement put the South Yorkshire area at such a disadvantage that its part in the coal trade to London fell into decline. Seven years later, having failed to get the agreement rescinded, the Great Northern reduced its rates by directing the South Yorkshire coal trains over a shorter route: but as soon as it did so the Midland also reduced its rates, and throughout the subsequent cuts it was the Midland which kept in the lead as the cheaper carrier. At the height of the dispute the Great Northern had reduced its rates from South Yorkshire to King's Cross from eight shillings and fourpence (42p) to five and threepence (26p) a ton but by 1872, when both companies had realised the folly of competitive price-cutting, it had returned to seven shillings and elevenpence (40p) per ton.[27] Neither company was the outright winner in the rates war. The Great Northern eventually built its line through the Midlands coalfield, from Colwick near Nottingham to Derby and Burton, with branches up the mining valleys. But by the time that was finished the Midland had achieved the far greater coup of opening its new London terminus at St Pancras. And on either side of the approach tracks to the new station it built coal drops, emblematic of the position it had secured in the trade.

Regardless of their squabbles, the combined effect of increased traffic on the Great Northern and the Midland, and on other lines, was to place the railways at the forefront of London's coal supply. Rail deliveries exceeded sea-borne deliveries for the first time in 1867.[28] But it would be a mistake to think that this triumph was conclusive, for already the sea carriers of coal were equipping themselves to meet the rail competition. In 1852 the steam-powered collier *John Bowes* was launched, capable of making a round trip from Tyneside to London in five days carrying about twice the tonnage of a sailing collier. A decade later, over a quarter of the coal brought to London by sea came in steam colliers.[29] Much of the advantage of faster journey times and larger loads would have been lost if unloading had still been by the customary labour-intensive methods. But these too were gradually superseded by the introduction of hydraulic wharf cranes, and by the use of steam cranes on floating derricks which could transfer coal into lighters further down the Thames.

The sea-borne traders were always at an advantage in supplying bulk deliveries to Thames-side factories and gas works, and so benefitted as the gas industry built new works along the river. They also always had a captive market in the steamships requiring bunkerage in the Port of London. Taken together, the effect of more efficient equipment and an expanding market put the sea-borne tonnage in the ascendant once again: more coal came by sea than by rail between the late 1890s and the outbreak of the First World War.[30]

This successful retaliation by the sea carriers of coal was made all the easier by the fact that the railways were encumbered by equipment that was increasingly out of date. The inter-related problems of the size of the waggons and the capacity of the coal-handling facilities made it hard for railway companies to forsake their established methods, as was nowhere better illustrated than at King's Cross. The coal drops in the goods yard had all been designed for small capacity waggons, carrying small loads destined for domestic consumption. The best way to economise in dealing with such traffic would have been to introduce larger waggons – of 15, 20 or even 30 ton capacity – for, as the Americans had shown, a short train of large waggons paid much better than a long train of small ones.[31] But if such waggons could not be accommodated on the drops, or in the loading bays at the collieries, it was worthless to make that change. To the immense frustration of many railway commentators, companies such as the Great Northern by and large retained their old equipment. The coal trains which rumbled down the main line to London between the wars, and indeed even later, were little different from those which had inaugurated the trade at King's Cross in 1851. One end result of this conservatism has been the survival of buildings and equipment which are now highly valued historically, but it is hard to deny that they exemplify a backward-looking frame of mind in the railway that continued to use them for so long.

FOOTNOTES

1 Ralph Davis, *The Rise of the English Shipping Industry in the Seventeenth and Eighteenth Centuries*, (1962), 209; B.R. Mitchell, *British Historical Statistics*, (1988), 245.
2 Roger Finch, *Coals From Newcastle*, (1973), 143–52; Simon Vale, 'Total Factor Productivity in the English Shipping Industry: The NE Coal Trade 1700–1800', *Economic Hist. Rev.*, XXXIX (August 1986), 358–65.
3 Quoted in Roger Finch, op.cit., 133.
4 Jack Simmons, *The Railway in Town and Country 1830–1914*, (1986), 42–43; Raymond Smith, *Sea Coal for London*, (1961), 276.
5 *Herapath's Journal*, 25 Feb 1854, 194.
6 Public Record Office. RAIL 236/273; Joseph Cubitt's Reports on Works, 7 April 1851.
7 R.C. Despard, 'Description of the Improvement on the Second Division of the River Lea Navigation; with Remarks on the Position of Canals Generally, in Reference to the Development of their Resources', *Minutes of the Proceedings of the Institution of Civil Engineers*, XVII (1857–58), 395.
8 RAIL 236/27; GNR Board Minutes, 9 Aug 1859 and 26 June 1860.
9 *London Exhibited*, (1851), 812. I am most grateful to Denis Smith and Malcolm Tucker for drawing this description to my attention.
10 Seymour Clarke, General Manager of the Great Northern Railway, in evidence to the Royal Commission on Railways, *Parl. Papers*, 1867, XXVIII.I, QQ12,660; 12,724.

11 RAIL 236/532: Conversion of Old Coal Shed into Goods Shed, 28–29.
12 RAIL 236/608/5: Letter to the Chairman of the GNR from Samuel Plimsoll, 23 Aug 1856; *Colliery Guardian*, 27 Feb 1858, 137.
13 *Herapath's Journal*, 30 June 1860, 639–40.
14 *Parl. Papers* 1867, op.cit., QQ12, 672–73; RAIL 236/283/4: Cessation of Coal Business by GNR.
15 *Herapath's Journal*, 2 Sep 1854, 890–91; David Masters, *The Plimsoll Mark* (1955), 45–50.
16 *The Times*, 10 Feb 1844, 4.
17 RAIL 236/80: GNR Executive Committee, 8 July 1856.
18 *Colliery Guardian*, 16 Jan 1858, 41.
19 RAIL 236/283/25; Samuel Plimsoll Special Train.
20 Patent No. 2909, 21 Dec 1859.
21 RAIL 236/305/20: Plimsoll's Experimental Coal Drops.
22 RAIL 236/295/12.
23 RAIL 236/587: Tonnage Book of the GNR Coal Depot.
24 *Engineering*, 26 Apr 1867, 417, reprinted in the *Colliery Guardian*, 5 Oct 1867, 306.
25 Quoted in Masters, op.cit., 200.
26 J. Wrottesley, *The Great Northern Railway* I (1979), 156.
27 *Colliery Guardian*, 2 Aug 1872, 125.
28 Raymond Smith, op.cit., 276.
29 Roger Finch, op.cit., 166–67; William J. Hausman, 'The English Coastal Trade 1891–1910: How Rapid was Productivity Growth?', *Economic Hist. Rev.*, XL (Nov 1987), 595.
30 Raymond Smith, op.cit., 339–40.
31 George Paish, *The British Railway Position* (1902), 27–35, 120–21.

CHAPTER SEVEN

King's Cross: History in the Making

Michael Hunter

Redevelopment. This has been the obvious future for the railway lands to the north and west of King's Cross and St Pancras stations ever since the scale of goods marshalling there began to enter its terminal decline. Yet this decline is itself a perhaps surprisingly recent phenomenon. This area was virtually ignored in the planning process for London in the aftermath of the war, when bomb damage had left more immediate priorities for large-scale rebuilding and development. In the County of London Plan of 1943, for instance, the railway lands are clearly demarcated as just that: a goods-handling area.[1] There was a proposal in 1946 to rebuild King's Cross station itself, and comparable schemes – involving both King's Cross and St Pancras – were to surface again in the 1960s:[2] fortunately, however, nothing came of these. Throughout these years, both the stations and the areas adjacent to them were left alone, continuing to serve their traditional functions.

In the 1950s and 1960s, however, declining demand for the coal which had always been the main staple of the goods yards, and the increasing shift of goods away from the railways onto the roads, led to a diminishing amount of activity in the whole goods yard complex. This trend was accelerated by the general rationalisation of the resources of British Railways presided over by Dr Beeching, and it became increasingly apparent that the old marshalling yards could be put to different, more socially relevant or commercially productive, use.

This did not only apply to the railway lands which form the subject of the proposed development that is being discussed as this book goes to press. It was equally true of a series of adjacent sites, for in a sense the so-called 'King's Cross railway lands' represent only the residue of a larger area (see map on p126). To the north, this included the land between the North London Line and Agar Grove, and, to the west, that separating the current development site from the street now called Pancras Way. Further south, there was the site between St Pancras and Somers Town fronting Euston Road, the former Somers Town goods depot. Between them, these made the area devoted to goods-handling facilities more than twice as large as the rump that the current redevelopment covers. Indeed, this itself might raise questions as to whether the site for which plans are currently being formulated – which partly comprises the last, if the largest, of such goods-handling areas and partly the area south of Goods Way which is quite different in character – should be treated as a unitary entity at all.

78. An aerial view of the King's Cross area.

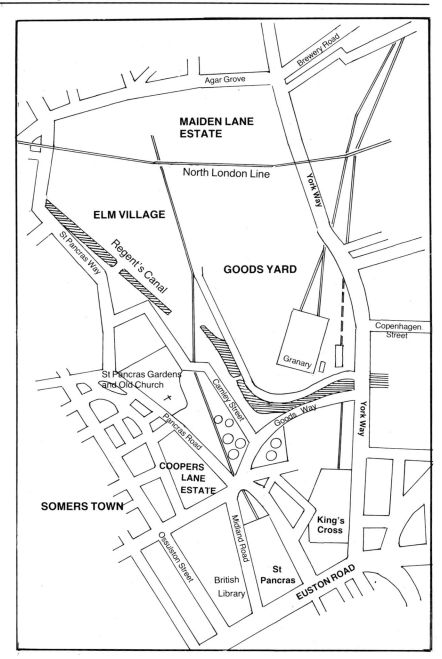

79. Map of the King's Cross area showing the railway areas which have now been redeveloped for other uses or else are still semi-derelict.

Gradually, in the 1960s and early 1970s, the other sites were picked off and redeveloped, the purposes to which they were put reflecting the priorities of metropolitan and municipal planning in those years. Thus the land adjacent to Agar Grove passed into the ownership of the London Borough of Camden and was devoted to council housing – becoming the Maiden Lane estate – while the same occurred with the area to the west of Pancras Road and north of Phoenix Street, now called Coopers Lane. Elm Village by Pancras Way, on the other hand, became a mixed development of Housing Association and private housing, while the rest of the land to the west of the lines out from St Pancras, both north and south of the North London Line, was devoted to light industrial use.

Lastly, despite vociferous opposition from those who would have liked to see it, too, devoted to public housing, in 1975 the then Secretary of State for the Environment, Anthony Crosland, declared that the former Somers Town goods depot adjacent to St Pancras station in the Euston Road should become the site of the British Library. This thus ended two decades of uncertainty over the future of the site previously earmarked for the new library, the streets south of the British Museum in Bloomsbury.[3]

By the late 1970s, therefore, the area covered by the current redevelopment schemes had already been demarcated. Then, as now, the land was owned predominantly by British Rail and the National Freight Corporation, with subsidiary holdings by the British Waterways Board, North Thames Gas and Camden Council – a balance itself reflecting the transport activities to which the neighbourhood had formerly been devoted. There was, however, something of a gap in active planning for the site at this stage, perhaps partly because grandiose schemes were under consideration, such as an Inner London airport terminus at its southern end. Meanwhile, priorities and strategies for municipal planning were rapidly changing, particularly in the early years of the Thatcher government. The trend was now away from the large-scale public-oriented projects typical of the post-war years and well-exemplified by the developments in adjacent areas that have already been described, towards the involvement of private capital and enterprise, which, as we shall see, has dominated recent discussion of the site. This was combined with increasing government pressure on British Rail to comply with its statutory obligation to obtain the maximum financial return for its redundant property and land.

During the intervening years, various minor – if symbolically significant – developments occurred on the part of the site north of Goods Way. The Regent's Canal had already been declared a Conservation Area in 1974, and in 1983, as a means of safeguarding its character, Conservation Area status was extended to the buildings lining its banks (in 1986 the Conservation Area was further extended to include virtually the whole of the goods depot on the north bank of the canal within the railway lands; in the same year, the four most decorative gasometers were listed). In 1982–3 plans were even formulated for creating a museum in the goods depot, though nothing came of this. More significantly, in 1983 an area of derelict land lying across the canal to the west of the goods depot was made available to the London Wildlife Trust as a nature reserve, and within the next year the Camley Street Natural Park took shape: over the intervening years this strip of lush vegetation in the shadow of the gasometers has become a powerful symbol of the potential for natural regeneration in the inner city.

Apart from these initiatives the main focus of attention in the late 1970s and early 1980s was the area south of Goods Way, which was the subject of active concern by the Greater London Council from 1977 onwards. The GLC's aim was both to improve the transport interchange that dominates this neighbourhood and to upgrade its economic and environmental character as a whole. In 1978, a public exhibition was mounted displaying different options for the locality, and over the next few years much work went into devising strategies

80. The Camley Street Natural Park, 1990.

for it, which materialised in a lavishly produced 'Draft Action Area Plan' in 1985. Since the GLC was abolished the following year, there was not much time to implement the policies outlined in this document, but the Council had already begun to provide the facilities which the area was deemed to need at Battlebridge Basin, just across York Way in the Borough of Islington: here the GLC encouraged the rehabilitation and replacement of buildings on the canal to provide industrial and light-industrial premises and housing. In addition, just before its abolition, the GLC declared a substantial area around King's Cross a Conservation Area in March 1986.

We now move to August 1987, when the development proposals that have since dominated interest in the site first came to public notice. How long before this the major landowners of the site had been actively considering its future use it is impossible to be sure — it may have been months, if not years. But for our purposes what matters is that at this point a confidential report on its potential for comprehensive redevelopment, dated June 1987, was leaked to the *Architects Journal*. Before the month was out the story was picked up, first by local papers like the *Camden New Journal* and then by national ones such as the *Sunday Times* and *Guardian*.

The story that came to light itself confirmed the type of development that had come to seem appropriate by the late 1980s, namely one dominated by the construction of offices. Ironically, between the late 1970s and the mid 1980s the GLC had actually shifted its priorities away from office provision in this area, on the grounds that offices built along the Pentonville Road in Islington had failed to be let.[4] But the experience of comparable developments like the Docklands and Broadgate — on the fringes of the City — had made it clear that King's Cross was a potential site for a comparable highly profitable, speculative development. In fact, it was for the developers of Broadgate, Rosehaugh Stanhope, that the confidential memorandum leaked to the *Architects Journal* was prepared, and in this the analogy with Broadgate was specifically made.[5]

It is easy to see why King's Cross seemed so attractive. Here was a site four times larger than Broadgate and twice as large even as Canary Wharf, the prime business centre in the Docklands; it was also ideally placed between the City of London and the West End. It is not surprising that, in the subsequent months, it was repeatedly referred to in superlatives – as 'the most exciting and challenging development opportunity presently being contemplated in Britain', if not 'one of the most significant inner city development sites in the world'.[6]

The local response was immediate. In August 1987, a Railway Lands Community Development Group was set up (it later added 'King's Cross' to its name). On 17 September 1987 it organised a public meeting at a local community theatre, which was packed and at which local interest in and apprehension about the site were clearly apparent. Even from the letter that the Group sent the *Camden New Journal* to announce its formation, it was obvious that a deep conflict existed between the priorities of the landowners and putative developers of the site and those of local people. The letter warned darkly of the risk that the provision of offices, luxury housing and specialist shopping would result in the loss of Council homes and bring about a change in the electoral nature of the area. It urged Camden Council, as planning authority, to consider its priorities for the site carefully and to learn from the experiences of other local authorities who had faced similar developments in the past.[7] Implicit was a potential confrontation between the objectives of Camden, as a Labour-controlled Council, and the priorities of those who had by this time taken the initiative over the site.

Camden Council did, indeed, take the matter up swiftly, making up for its lack of a proper strategy for the railway lands hitherto by convening a whole series of meetings at which local people were consulted, and then rapidly drafting a Planning Brief for the site. This document, *The King's Cross Railway Lands: a Community Planning Brief*, appeared in January 1988: it was thus produced in as many months as it had taken the GLC years to produce *its* Draft Local Plan for the King's Cross Action Area. The Camden Brief set out the Council's priorities for the site, stressing the need to improve the transport interchange, and to provide for the housing, employment and recreation of local people. It also emphasised the importance of respecting the character of the area and of safeguarding local and strategic views. The document was cautious on the question of how much office provision might be appropriate, stating that this must depend on a range of issues, including the scale of community benefits provided and the state of the market. It urged that the development should demonstrate how large-scale inner-city regeneration could be achieved through co-operation rather than confrontation. This summary of the Council's objectives was accompanied by a series of annexes giving information on such questions as the leisure facilities and the proportion of different types of housing that would be deemed acceptable, and the historic buildings and strategic views which deserved protection.

The autumn of 1987 saw two further developments concerning King's Cross as a centre of public transport. One was the tragic fire in November in which 31 people died: this made improvements to the transport interchange there more necessary than ever, while the subsequent Fennell report into the disaster stressed that safety considerations should play a more integral role in planning than hitherto. The second was the fact that, although as recently as March 1987 British Rail had categorically denied before a House of Lords Committee that it was feasible to make King's Cross a terminal for the Channel Tunnel, it now decided that, on the contrary, this was an ideal site for just this purpose.[8] As a result the confidential brief which British Rail prepared for putative developers of the site in October 1987 included an instruction to incorporate such facilities in any scheme.

Four developers were invited to submit plans which complied with British Rail's requirements for the site, and they did so in December that year. Then, in

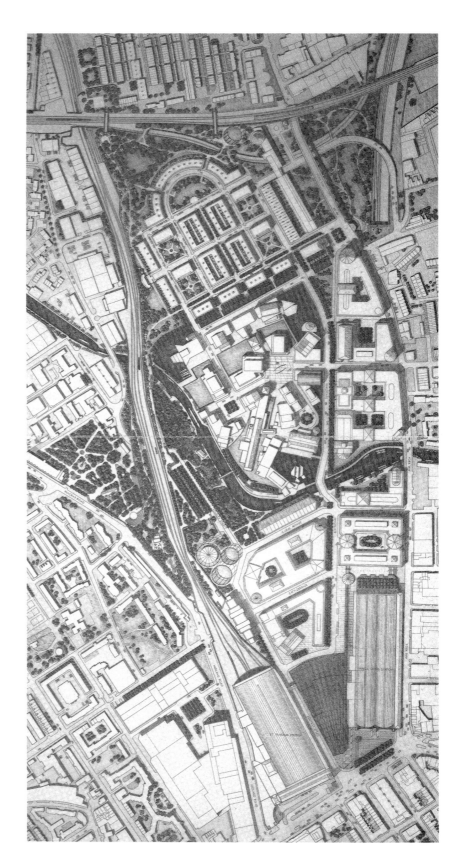

81. *The scheme designed by Skidmore, Owings and Merrill for the London Regeneration Consortium.*

January 1988, it was announced that these would be exhibited to the public: the idea was that by inspecting the different potential schemes the public could learn what was proposed for the area and help the landowners decide between the different options. By now, the competing developers had been reduced to two, one of which was the recently-formed London Regeneration Consortium, a conglomerate comprising the National Freight Corporation, the largest minority landowner on the site, and Rosehaugh Stanhope: as noted above, the latter had already been active in the vast Broadgate development, while other schemes in which they were involved included Finsbury Avenue in the City and Stockley Park at Heathrow. Their rivals were Speyhawk/McAlpine, whose proposal to rehabilitate the Midland Grand Hotel at St Pancras was at this time painfully making its way through Camden Council's planning process; they had also undertaken major commercial developments elsewhere in the country.

The architects for Speyhawk/McAlpine were Yorke, Rosenberg and Mardell. London Regeneration Consortium, on the other hand, surprised everyone by offering two different schemes, one by the American architects, Skidmore, Owings and Merrill, the other by Norman Foster's Foster Associates, who had initially been brought in as subordinates to SOM, but who found that they disagreed so fundamentally about the layout of the site that they produced their own Masterplan for it. All three produced elaborate, coloured brochures illustrating their proposals, and LRC's material, in particular, was extraordinarily lavish: at this point it included an A2 leaflet which featured art photographs of a man walking his dog around the site. All of the publicity protested the good intentions of the developers and architects to make the new complex as beneficial for local people as for office-workers, sentiments which reached a climax in Foster Associates' submission, which saw the need for urban regeneration as 'desperately urgent for the tens of thousands of our citizens whose current fate is to lead out [sic] their lives in unbelievably inadequate and brutalising environments.'[9] Opinions of just how much the proposed scheme was likely to benefit such unfortunates will be discussed below.

The various plans displayed a number of common features, at least some of which evidently stemmed from the British Rail brief. All of them took for granted that the Great Northern Hotel would be demolished and replaced by a new structure, a circular brick pavilion in the YRM scheme, a glazed building like an airport terminal in the SOM and Foster plans. Behind were vistas of huge office blocks, some built over existing railway lines, and grandiose housing developments. All the schemes made provision for the retention of a handful of historic buildings, most of them in a kind of theme park north of the Regent's Canal.

Beyond this the schemes differed. YRM proposed a massive office development focussed on 'Grand Union Plaza' at the southern end of the site, overshadowing the great trainsheds of King's Cross and St Pancras; to the north was to be found 'Grand Union Park' surrounded by housing and, further north still, a business and science park linked to the southern end of the site by a specially constructed monorail. SOM postulated a similar large-scale office development at the southern end, but suggested the creation of 'Battlebridge Island' to the north of the canal, which was to be an area of mixed use and which seemed from the drawings to have quite an 'organic' feel to it; the northern end was given over to a residential development called 'Camden Fields', surrounded by an irregularly-shaped park.

Undoubtedly the most striking plan, if that which bore the least relationship to the existing topography of the site, was that of Foster Associates. This was dominated by a central oval park straddling the Regent's Canal, an imaginative concept said to be inspired by the major and minor green spaces strung out along the canal as it passed though London 'like beads on a string'. In addition,

Foster's scheme included a grandiloquent glazed vault placed slightly awkwardly between and behind the facades of King's Cross and St Pancras stations, which was presented as a gateway to the site as a whole. Both features earned extravagant plaudits from the architectural press, while Martin Pawley even found himself moved to hail Foster's proposed relocation of the listed gasometers to clear the way for his scheme as a 'stroke of bravura'.[10] Both features, however, have been widely criticised, the park by those opposed to the way in which it would truncate the existing group of historic buildings at the centre of the site, and the arched 'gateway' by those who saw it as trivialising the two great stations between which it was intended to stand.

Early in the summer of 1988 British Rail invited final, revised submissions from the two developers and then, on 2 June, proceeded to adjudicate in favour of London Regeneration Consortium, who had been perceived as the clear favourites throughout the exercise. Then, later in June, LRC declared that Foster Associates had been chosen as Masterplanners for the site in preference to Skidmore, Owings and Merrill and over the following months Foster Associates set to work to refine and modify their Masterplan. Revised versions of it produced in September and October were widely publicised in a further illustrated brochure published in November. At the same time a whole team of experts made detailed feasibility studies of different options for the site in the light of the engineering, structural and commercial constraints on development. Indeed, this injection of expertise arguably did something to offset what some had seen as a drawback about the original selection of Foster Associates as Masterplanners, in that they were architects whose experience lay in designing individual buildings rather than in the field of town planning.

Those with reservations about the development were also active. Perhaps most significant was the 'Social Audit' produced by Michael Edwards and Ellen Leopold of the Bartlett School of Architecture at University College London, which sought to prove that the developers' claims about the scale of development needed to give a viable profit were exaggerated. By working through a series of options for different quantities of housing and offices – from as few as 108,000 to as many as 685,000 square metres of offices and from 2910 to 8292 rooms of family housing – they argued that a massive profit might be made while devoting far less of the site to offices than the developers saw as desirable, perhaps 350,000 square metres, as against the 700,000 or more proposed by LRC, though opinions have differed on the reliability of these figures. The report also pointed out that, as a result of impending changes in local government finance, Camden as local authority was likely to lose rather than gain from the scheme.[11]

Meanwhile the King's Cross Railway Lands Community Development Group had a series of information gathering meetings with LRC, in the course of which the degree of disagreement between them became increasingly evident. Alternative visions of the site were displayed in a rather different way by the competition 'King's Cross 2000', launched by the Camden Town Area Committee in March 1988. In this, local schoolchildren were encouraged to offer their view of how the site should be developed: over 1000 participated and the exhibition of their work which took place in November of that year showed that some of them were rather good Masterplanners, with a refreshing directness reflected in captions to details of their proposals like 'Expensive Flats'.

There were also initiatives by those who considered that the development as proposed was unduly destructive of the historic buildings on the site. The Victorian Society issued an illustrated leaflet, *Opportunity or Calamity: the King's Cross Railway Lands Development*. The Camden Civic Society organised a public meeting on the subject and produced a series of discussion documents. Most authoritatively of all, in November 1988 English Heritage published a definitive inventory of architectural and industrial features within the area covered

82. Prince Charles meeting children who took part in the 'King's Cross 2000' competition.

by the development, an epitome of which concludes this volume.

From the conservationist point of view, one episode which received a good deal of publicity over the summer of 1988 was something of an own goal on the part of the developers and landowners. For, just as spokesmen for LRC were assuring interested parties at the meeting organised by Camden Civic Society that no building would be touched until its future had been fully discussed, bulldozers were reducing one historic structure on the site, the former potato market near York Way, to rubble. It turned out that the demolition had been authorised by a local manager in British Rail Property Board, unbeknown to LRC; it was stopped as soon as the furore over it began. But by this time the building was irreparably damaged, and matters were made worse by the fact that no-one had even bothered to check whether anything of value had been left in it, with the result that, after demolition was halted, significant records concerning the Victorian potato trade were found exposed to the rain in the attics. The whole episode did little to add to confidence in the development partners, not least since, in their publicity leaflet about the site, LRC had actually accompanied a photograph of the potato market with the caption: 'A more fitting role for many of these fine buildings and beautiful spaces will emerge during the process of negotiation, consultation and design.'

Despite such setbacks, LRC remained active in promoting its scheme and informing the public about it. In July 1988 there was an open day in the goods yard, complete with exhibitions, stalls and even tours around the site in open-topped buses. In addition, LRC converted the Goods Offices into their headquarters, renaming the building 'Regeneration House', and a portakabin outside was made into a permanent exhibition centre. Then, at the end of November, LRC collaborated with Camden Council in a 'King's Cross Exchange' at which the developers sought to conduct a frank and full discussion of the scheme with the local community. The weekend comprised a mixture of workshops, at which detailed aspects of the scheme were discussed, and public meetings. The most exciting of the latter was a debate chaired by the

83. The ruined potato market.

television presenter, Vincent Hannah, at which broader issues arising from the development were aired, often with some acrimony.

The weekend almost exactly coincided with the lodging in Parliament of British Rail's Private Bill authorising the construction of a Channel Tunnel terminal at King's Cross. The details in this confirmed what had been leaked in the local press over the previous months about the scale of the proposed new station and its likely impact on the locality. As already noted, the provision of such a station had been part of British Rail's confidential brief to the developers a year earlier. Whereas at that point the underground station which it was proposed to build diagonally beneath the King's Cross trainshed had been relatively modest in scale, revisions to operational requirements meant that by the time the Bill was lodged it had almost doubled in size. In addition, an alignment had been chosen which, though doing less damage to houses in neighbouring parts of Islington than might otherwise have been the case, involved the total destruction of the Camley Street Natural Park.

Not surprisingly, the result was a further burst of public outrage, expressed by a barrage of petitioning against the British Rail Bill. (It should be explained that the same archaic procedure which allowed railway works to be authorised by private bills also sanctioned opposition to them through petitions written to a set formula.) Initially, 282 petitions were lodged, and, though half were disallowed by the Court of Referees after being challenged by British Rail, this still left a formidable body of opposition to the proposals. The Select Commit-

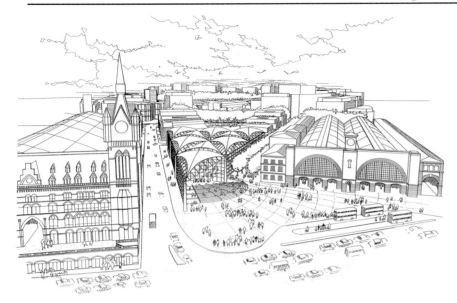

84. Norman Foster's proposed building to replace the Great Northern Hotel, between King's Cross and St Pancras stations.

tee appointed to deal with the Bill began to sit in the summer of 1989, when thirteen days' evidence was heard. Though due to recommence after the recess, however, proceedings were twice postponed due to mounting uncertainty over British Rail's plans for the rail link from the Channel Tunnel to London, caused by the government's insistence that this should not be dependent on public subsidy. They finally resumed in December, continuing through the early months of 1990 to reach a total of 51 days of hearings, a number almost without precedent. In the course of this a range of evidence was heard as to whether the Channel Tunnel terminus should be located at King's Cross, and about its likely impact. The promoters of the Bill faced opposition from Camden and Islington Councils, conservationist bodies and representatives of local groups and residents. The Committee's decision was further delayed by a government announcement in June 1990, which threw greater doubt than ever on the viability of a high speed rail link. Only in July was the Bill finally approved, though with significant modifications, particularly in response to conservationist concerns. But the measure still has to face committee proceedings in the House of Lords, and uncertainty concerning the outcome could well have severe implications for the railway lands development as a whole.

This was one problem that the developers had not foreseen at the outset. Another was the discovery that St Bartholomew's Hospital, as a former freeholder of some of the goods yard land who had been bought out at the time the Great Northern Railway had been built here, had a residual claim to repurchase the land at the 19th century price if it ceased to be used for railway purposes. This matter was subsequently to reach the High Court, and the figures discussed in connection with the competing claims – running into tens of millions of pounds – indicate the current value of land which Barts originally sold for some £50,000.

We must now return to April 1989, when LRC's planning application was at last submitted. Though the application itself comprised only a map of the site dividing it into sections, with a schedule of proposed uses and storey heights, it was accompanied by documentation of every conceivable aspect of the development and its likely impact on the locality. The Foster plan as shown in

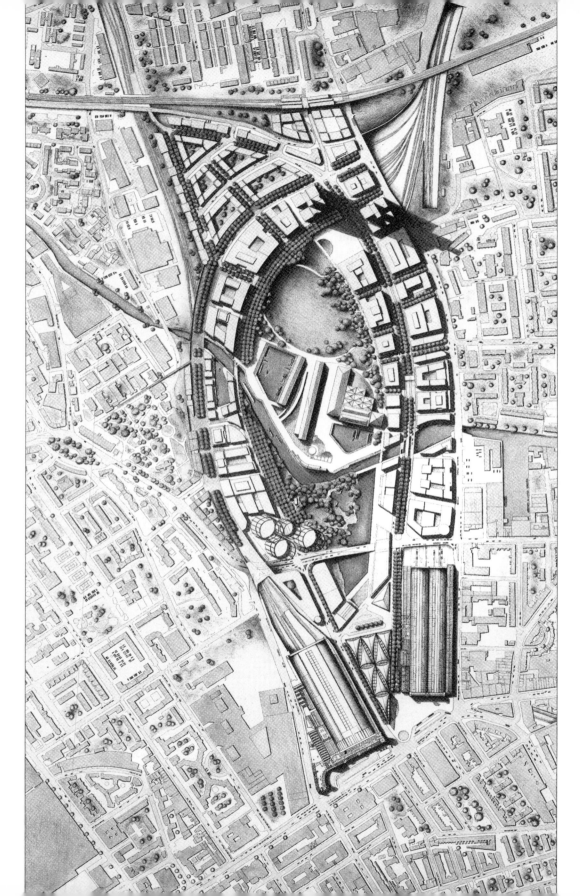

this illustrative material still bore a recognisable similarity to the original scheme as exhibited in the British Rail competition over a year earlier. In particular, the oval central park still remained, as did the radiating avenues of office blocks and housing. On the other hand, the design for the southern end of the site had been extensively modified, partly because of the needs imposed by the increasing scale of British Rail's railway works, but also because of the widespread disquiet about the glazed arch that had originally been proposed to replace the Great Northern Hotel between the two stations. In May 1989 a subsidiary planning application was submitted for this concourse, and by this time it had dwindled to so modest a building that it began to seem difficult to understand why it could not be combined with the retention of the existing hotel.

As the application was digested by the Council and by the public, it became apparent that a fundamental incompatibility existed between the wishes of the developers and those of local people. Foster's scheme remained predominant-ly an introspective 'Office City' with disappointingly little to offer those who lived on and around the site. If views on this point may have been irreconcil-able, it is perhaps more surprising how little the developers had done to placate interest groups such as conservationists. For, despite protests that these had made from the start about the brutal way in which the proposed development treated the historically important group of surviving buildings in the goods yard, these cries seemed to have fallen on almost wholly deaf ears. When a second King's Cross Exchange was held by Camden Council in July 1989 disillusionment on the part of the public and the local authority was evident. At

85. The current redevelopment plan of the London Regeneration Consortium.

86. The 'King's Cross Exchange' in action at Camden Town Hall.

this point, Tony Dykes, Leader of Camden Council, went on record as saying that the planning application as submitted was 'totally unacceptable'[12] – a view endorsed by his officers and fellow councillors two months later.

As a result the developers submitted a completely new application to Camden in October, which is under consideration as this book goes to press. This scheme responded to criticism of its predecessor by significantly increasing the acreage devoted to housing, though it remains to be seen whether the extra provision is of either sufficient quantity or appropriate type to satisfy Camden. On the other hand, the office content was reduced by only 5%, room instead being found for it by the inclusion of two 40–45 storey tower-blocks in the north-east corner of the site. These and other modifications entailed the abandonment of the oval shape for the park in favour of a beak-like physiognomy, while a further change brought areas of water to within one block of the trainsheds. Fundamentally, however, the scheme remained similar to its predecessors, and it seems unlikely that Camden Council will give it permission unless much more extensive modifications are made.

Quite different approaches were shown by alternative plans for the site which emerged in the first half of 1990. Those exhibited at the Shaw Theatre in the Euston Road early in April were suggestive but somewhat provisional. More significant was the announcement later that month that Martin Clarke, a developer in Camden Town, had given financial backing to a team of professional planners and architects who aimed to devise a completely different scheme, complying with Camden's original planning brief and reflecting local interests. A 'Planning for Real' exercise was undertaken with the King's Cross Railway Lands Community Development Group, involving a series of public meetings from which a 'People's Brief' for the site was to be produced as a basis for a new draft Masterplan. What will come of these initiatives is unclear but, as with the continuing uncertainty over the King's Cross Railways Bill, yet another element is added to an already complicated situation.

This essay was written while events still unfolded and it will be illuminating eventually to look back on the affair in retrospect. There is no reason to doubt that, at the outset, London Regeneration Consortium genuinely believed that it should be possible to have the best of both worlds – a highly profitable development, which, through consultation and research, would do as much as was economically viable to meet the wishes of local people. They apparently presumed that much of the opposition would come from noisy activists, and that if they could get behind these and talk to the 'real' community, they would find that most people supported the proposals. In this they seem to have been mistaken. Though the first of the lavish broadsheets that they issued bore the headline '81% say Yes', it turned out that all this meant was that 81% of those questioned about the scheme were in favour of some form of redevelopment of the railway lands. Yet barely half of this number – only 41% – wanted offices as the developers proposed, as was divulged in rather smaller print below, and this represented the lowest percentage in favour of any of the possible options included, with housing and recreational facilities respectively scoring 90% and 87%.[13]

On the other hand, there are also factors at play which advantage the developer. One is the general shift in political climate which has encouraged office-led development on sites which would almost certainly have been devoted to public-oriented schemes in the post-war years. In addition, LRC have from the outset been favoured by an openly admitted reluctance on the part of Camden Council, hamstrung by financial stringency, to run the risk of going to a public inquiry. Moreover, the possibility has throughout existed that the Secretary of State for the Environment may call the application in on the grounds that it will have a major impact on neighbouring Islington as well as Camden, and that it is of too great importance for London as a whole for

Camden Council to deal with it. This would clearly tend to favour the developers even if they suffered a lengthy delay in the process.

In chronicling the complex story of the development plans and their vicissitudes, this essay may have appeared somewhat negative. But this is not its intention. One thing on which virtually everyone can agree is that the redevelopment of this site is not only inevitable but highly desirable: it is amazing that so many acres of land so close to the centre of London should have been derelict for so long. A site of this magnitude ought to be able to provide a remarkable opportunity to fulfil both local and metropolitan needs in a concept that is architecturally exciting while also retaining and enhancing what is best about the locality. One would naturally expect views to differ on the desirable mix between different kinds of uses – housing, offices, recreation and light industry. Yet it is hard to accept that the widespread local disquiet about the scheme is entirely due to an inward looking conservatism. Discussion of the plans for the railway lands has coincided with public debate over the Prince of Wales's *Vision of Britain*, in which he commented on this site: 'The opportunities at King's Cross are phenomenal. Improving conditions for the surrounding community should be a priority, and careful consultations are essential to avoid just another rehash of so many of London's recent developments.'[14] More generally, there is much to be learnt in the local context from his plea for sensitivity in dealing with historic buildings and environments and for a more human scale in development and design. Contrary to the presumption of his critics, this need not produce either bad architecture or bad planning. King's Cross could yet show the potential for a redevelopment that is exciting without being overpowering, viable without being socially exclusive, imaginative without being wantonly destructive. *That* is what the railway lands really need.

FOOTNOTES

1   J.H. Forshaw and Patrick Abercrombie, *County of London Plan*, (1943), e.g. maps facing 28, 70, 120.
2   *The Builder*, 22 Feb 1946; *Daily Telegraph*, 26 Aug 1966.
3   Philip Davies, 'Change for King's Cross', *Illustrated London News*, Oct 1975, 43–5.
4   *King's Cross and St Pancras. GLC Action Area Draft Local Plan*, (1985), 13.
5   *Architects Journal*, 5 Aug 1987.
6   *Grand Union Plaza*, Speyhawk McAlpine leaflet for the British Rail competition (Feb 1988); LRC advertisement, *Hampstead and Highgate Express*, 1 July 1988.
7   *Camden New Journal*, 10 Sept 1987.
8   Andy Gliniecki, 'Battle of Waterloo', *Time Out*, 27 Jan 1988.
9   Foster Associates, *Master Plan Proposals for the King's Cross Railway Lands* (Feb 1988).
10 *The Guardian*, 23 June 1988.
11 Bartlett School of Architecture and Planning, *Alternatives for King's Cross: Report on a Pilot Social Audit*, (Nov 1988), esp. Appendix 3. See also Ellen Leopold, 'The Impact of Proposals to Develop the King's Cross Railway Lands', *Local Economy*, May 1989, 17–28.
12 *Camden New Journal*, 13 July 1989.
13 *King's Cross Extra*, No. 1 (Nov 1988).
14 The Prince of Wales, *A Vision of Britain*, (1989), 62.

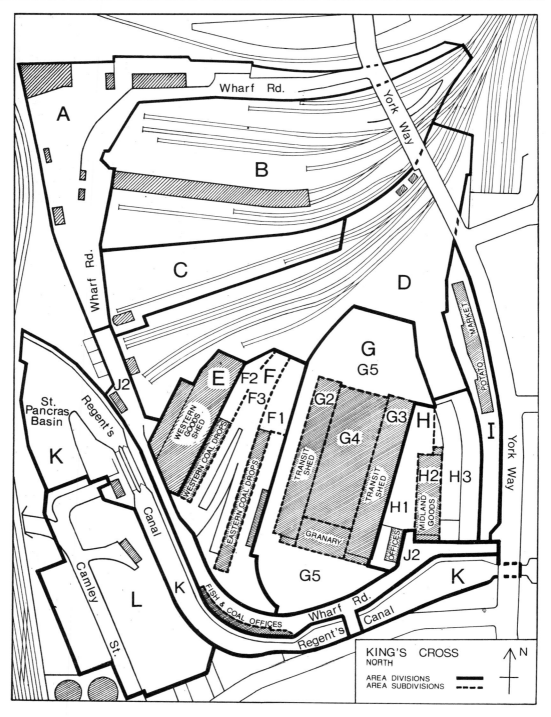

87. Key plan, north of the canal.

CHAPTER EIGHT

The English Heritage Inventory of the King's Cross Site

Stephen Duckworth and Barry Jones

This inventory is a shortened version of a report prepared for English Heritage in October 1988. It describes the buildings and artefacts on the King's Cross site as they appeared at that time. The only buildings which are not covered are the two main line stations and their associated hotels, which have been discussed elsewhere.

The inventory is divided into twenty-six sections corresponding to the areas shown on the accompanying maps. Those sections which are particularly rich in historical evidence have been further subdivided. At the end of the inventory are two thematic summaries covering roof structures and street furniture.

Throughout 'Humber' refers to the map accompanying William Humber's paper in the *Minutes of the Proceedings of the Institution of Civil Engineers*, XXV, 1865–66, and 'Goad' refers to Goad's Insurance Plans Vol. XII (1891), as revised in 1939.

AREA A: NORTH-WEST CORNER OF THE SITE
This area comprises Wharf Road, which flanks the goods yard to the north and west, and assorted buildings adjacent to the road.

FEATURES
1. Warehouse
This unusual brick building at the far north end consists of a central section of seven bays, flanked to the west by a rectangular shed with single-ridged clerestory roof, and to the east by a low, square block with a hipped slate roof. An irregular toilet block stands at the south-west corner.

The main feature of interest is the inverted-hipped timber roof over the central section, which is supported by a single colonnade of cast-iron columns.

2. Former Locomotive Superintendent's House
This is located adjacent to the site of the King's Cross 'Top Shed' steam locomotive depot, closed in 1963 and now demolished. The house is L-shaped in plan with a hipped roof. There is a bay window on the south elevation to the side of the original main doorway.

88. Former Locomotive superintendent's house (A2).

3. Miscellaneous Buildings
Several typical goods yard huts remain in this area. They are constructed of brick and/or concrete and have Welsh slate roofs. There is also a small single storey brick warehouse.

AREA B: CONCRETE DEPOT AND SIDINGS
Unlike most of the goods sidings, this area remains in use and some of the sidings have recently been relaid. Its southern half partially overlies the site of the GNR locomotive depot and the short-lived Midland Railway Roundhouse to the east of this. The northern half of the site was initially a coal stacking ground, later used for general sidings. Much of the south-western part of this area has been used for dumping spoil.

FEATURES
1. Long Shed
A substantial shed covers two railway lines and a central platform. The shed is open to the north and at both ends and has a gabled roof carried on fabricated I-section pillars

and beams. The roof structure has timber queen-post trusses with tie-beams consisting of two lengths of timber scarf-jointed below the apex. The trusses project beyond the supporting columns and the hybrid structure suggests considerable re-use of materials.

2. Inclined Viaduct
This red brick viaduct formerly carried the line giving access to the Caledonian Market above the Copenhagen tunnel. Its arches contain various BR workshops, many still in use.

AREA C: SITE OF GNR LOCOMOTIVE DEPOT
The site of the former GNR 'Top Shed' steam locomotive depot is buried beneath an expanse of builder's rubble between the present concrete depot and the disused Freightliner terminal.

FEATURES
1. Turntable Site
The outline of an infilled turntable pit is clearly visible at the east end of the area.

2. Water Softening Plant
This is the major surviving relic of the locomotive depot. Its purpose was to treat the hard local water to prevent the build-up of scale in steam locomotive boilers.

An irregular, octagonal building of blue engineering brick and concrete supports a water tank of riveted pressed steel panels. This replaced a circular tank (seen in aerial photographs taken in 1957).

AREA D: FREIGHTLINER DEPOT AND GOODS YARD SIDINGS
This area covers the site of the former coal stacking sidings and the sidings giving access to the main goods yard buildings in areas E to I.

FEATURES
1. Shunters' Huts
Located just to the west of the York Way viaduct are two rows of shunters' huts. They are of various dates and styles, mostly of brick construction with slate roofs.

2. Original Maiden Lane Bridge
This narrow section of the brick viaduct carrying York Way matches the original extent of the goods yard sidings. The stock brick arches spring from abutments faced with dressed stone quoins, a refinement lacking in the later northern section of the viaduct.

3. Low Level Goods Shed Ramp
A single railway line descends between retaining walls of blue engineering brick to give access to the lower level of the western goods shed. The walls are surmounted by railings with cast-iron stanchions lettered 'Richards and Son, Leicester'.

4. Offices on Wharf Road
These are shown on the 1865 Humber map, with a weighbridge located nearby. They are of ornamental yellow stock brick with a slate roof and are more elaborate than other small sheds on the site.

AREA E: WESTERN GOODS SHED
This was built abutting the western coal drops in 1897–99 on the site of the original coal and stone-handling basin. Initially it was used entirely for outward goods traffic, leaving the 1850 transit sheds for the use of inward traffic. However, these roles were reversed in 1938. Offices were provided over the shed along its western side.

FEATURES
1. Chronology of Construction
There are three distinct phases of construction: a southern section as described in 2 below, a northern section of coarsely-built timber, north-lit, sheds, and an intermediate section which closely matches the former and is probably close in date.

2. Internal Structure
At low level cast-iron columns and fabricated girders support a ceiling of concrete arches and lintels. Each of the columns bears an oval maker's mark 'W. Richards and Son, Makers, Leicester'. The two westerly colonnades have columns set at a lower level and each column carries a cast-iron extension to reach the uniform height of the roof girders. The extension pieces bear oval maker's marks 'Richards and Son'.

On the upper level the structures are of lighter construction, with fabricated pillars supporting transverse lattice girders. The latter divide the structure into transverse bays each of which has a gablet roof. Along the western side of the shed the pillars and girders are more substantial to support the offices above.

3. Wall Abutting the Western Coal Drops
The west wall of the coal drops was extended to perform a dual role as the eastern wall of the goods shed. The brick piers of the coal drop wall were strengthened by 'wrap-around' brickwork to support the weight of the new shed's roof and floor.

4. Rail Access to Lower Level
Railway lines in the lower level of the shed were accessed from the main sidings and yard via a single line incline between retaining walls. This cutting is now partially roofed by the shed's northern extensions, and provides additional storage space in the lower level warehousing.

5. Canal Bridge
The viaduct carrying Wharf Road incorporates the canal bridge over the former inlet to the coal and stone basin. The bridge consists of nine cast-iron beams supporting iron plates that carry the road surface. These details can be viewed from the lower level of the Western Shed along with the dressed stone quoins and cornices of the bridge abutments.

6. Overhead Offices
Offices for goods clerks were located along the north-west wall above the upper goods-handling floor. The offices have been substantially modernised with partition walls and a new suspended ceiling. Double-hung sash windows remain, as does the original composite roof structure. The roof trusses are simplified versions of those in the goods shed itself.

AREA F: THE COAL DROPS, LOW LEVEL YARD AND VIADUCTS

This area is located between the Granary and the western goods shed. It contains substantial evidence of an extremely important part of the GNR's goods traffic: the distribution of coal from the north-east and Yorkshire to the London market. It is considered here under three sub-headings.

AREA F1: THE EASTERN COAL DROPS

Built in 1851, this brick and cast-iron structure originally carried four high-level railway tracks from which waggons discharged coal into storage bins on a mezzanine floor above cart-loading bays. Longitudinal and transverse walls divided the structure into 48 cells within each of which two cast-iron columns and a cast-iron beam supported the timber coal storage bins.

A waggon traverser was provided at the southern end by which empty waggons were transferred to a wooden viaduct west of the coal drops.

Late in the 19th century the southern section was converted into a warehouse, leaving the northern bays for coal handling. These were badly damaged by fire in 1985, though the warehouse section survived undamaged.

FEATURES
1. Coal Chutes
Remains of the coal chutes can be found in two of the north-eastern bays. There are two different types of cast-iron 'jaw' and clear indications of the angled chute locations between the mezzanine floor joists. The 'jaws' are of a primitive nature, suggesting an early date, and their precise manner of operation is unclear.

2. Cast Iron Structure
Both the internal structure and external brick walls are supported by a simple framework of cast-iron columns and beams in each bay. The columns have a square plinth, simple moulded base and separately-cast cushion capital and abacus. The latter feature serves a primarily decorative function, and the full weight of the overlying structure is carried by the relatively slender head of the column shaft. The columns supporting the external brick walls are located in such a way that less than half the wall thickness is positioned above the column, leaving the remainder carried on the cast-iron beams of the internal structure.

The cast beams are of inverted T-section with integrally-cast joist footings on the upper edge. The warehouse conversion has left most of the cast-iron structure in situ except in a few of the western cells.

3. Traverser Evidence
The southern bay of the coal drops formerly housed the waggon traverser by which emptied waggons were removed sideways to be assembled into trains on an adjacent timber viaduct. This viaduct was subsequently replaced by the present brick structure to the west of the drops.

A cast-iron beam originally spanned the traverser opening on the west wall: this and its two pad stones remain in situ, as do two pad stones on the east wall. Several phases of brick infilling are also present at these positions.

4. Roofs (See section on roofs on p155)

5. Miscellaneous
(i) *Gasworks Viaduct*
The 1883 OS Map shows a second viaduct running along the eastern side of the coaldrops, crossing Wharf Road and the canal to enter the gasworks' retort houses. Evidence of this structure can be seen in the brickwork along the coal drops' eastern wall.

(ii) *Warehouse Crane*
A cast-iron hoisting arm is located alongside a taking-in door on the east elevation.

AREA F2: THE WESTERN COAL DROPS
The western coal drops were built in 1859–60 and, although only five years later than the eastern drops, they illustrate major developments in construction, in particular a much simplified method of carrying the high-level railway tracks using substantial cast-iron beams. A traverser and timber viaduct were provided as in the eastern coal drops.

The structure was converted to a general goods transit area when the western goods shed was built alongside in 1897–99. Three of the four tracks were replaced by a loading platform, the drops themselves converted to warehousing and a road viaduct was constructed on the south-east side to serve the new loading platform.

FEATURES
1. Coal Chutes and Cast Iron Beams
A single surviving line of rails is carried by a pair of fish-bellied cast-iron girders in each bay. These have projecting lugs along the lower flange which locate longitudinal timber baulks, carrying the rails. The beams are reinforced by timber raking struts, corbelled from the transverse walls dividing the bays.

Three additional pairs of beams support the higher level loading platform. These rest on substantial pad stones which have angled edges corresponding to the likely position of the original coal chutes.

It is likely that the surviving line of rails is at original height; the other three sets of cast-iron beams having been raised to support the platform. There are no substantial remains of the coal hoppers and chutes.

2. Traverser Evidence
As in the eastern coal drops the south bay was originally occupied by a traverser. An opening survives on the west wall, now reduced in height, but with the cast-iron beam remaining in place. The brickwork at this location also displays indication of several phases of alterations.

3. Miscellaneous
(i) *Loading Bay Canopy*
This is supported by steel cantilevered beams and ornate cast-iron brackets and has a serrated wooden valance of typical railway design.
(ii) *Crane Structure*
At the loading bay level one of the brick arches of the external walls has been replaced by a cast-iron beam. Adjacent to this are massive timber roof beams with pivots for former cranes.

4. ROOFS – see section on roofs on p155

AREA F3: LOW LEVEL YARD, STABLES AND VIADUCTS

This cobbled yard is spanned by three viaducts: one adjacent to each of the coal drops and a central one built to serve the Plimsoll coal drops on the opposite side of the canal. Stables occupy the arches beneath Wharf Road on the south and west side of the yard.

FEATURES

1. Stables

The arches beneath Wharf Road were used as stables and a few retain wooden stalling, ventilation slats and assorted tethering chains.

89. Stables beneath Wharf Road   (F3).

2. Viaducts

Both the central and eastern viaducts are built of blue engineering brick, the former having spans of reinforced concrete, the latter having blue brick arches. Both replace earlier timber structures. The original central structure was built in 1865–6 to give access to Samuel Plimsoll's coal drops, and its present replacement is of interest for its use of gradients and gravity to propel waggons to and from the drops, thus reducing the need for shunting and capstan work.

The road viaduct adjacent to the western coal drop is constructed of massive cast-iron columns and fabricated girders, the columns all bearing lettering 'Richards and Son, Makers, Leicester'.

3. Cast-Iron Fence Stanchions

Fence stanchions on the two western viaducts are all of identical design but bear raised lettering representing three periods of the yard's ownership with the initials GNR, LNER and BR present on different posts.

AREA G: THE GRANARY AND TRANSIT SHED COMPLEX

This substantial complex of structures contains several of the earliest and largest features of the GNR's goods facilities at King's Cross. It is considered under five sub-headings:

AREA G1: THE GRANARY

Along with the two transit sheds which flank it, the Granary is the primary feature of the goods interchange facilities. The building survives largely unaltered and in view of its importance the major features are described in detail.

FEATURES

1. Internal Frame and Roof Structure

The internal frame comprises cast-iron columns and beams with timber joists and floor surfaces. Each floor has 46 columns of a standard design, arranged in six colonnades each supporting a line of paired cast-iron beams running approximately east-west.

The timber roof makes considerable use of iron brackets and plates at the joints and has a Welsh slate cladding now covered by a layer of bitumen.

From the ground up to the fourth floor the column circumferences become progressively smaller. The column heights are a standard 2.4 metres except for those at ground floor which are all 4.1 metres high.

The cast-iron beams carry parallel longitudinal timber plates which hold the wooden floor joists. Between each colonnade there are wrought-iron tie-rods running transversely and linking the cast-iron beams.

On the fifth floor the columns are of two different heights, the higher ones in the two central colonnades supporting the roof structure, the lower columns forming two colonnades to either side. The latter support massive cast-iron beams that originally bore water tanks used in a low pressure hydraulic power system.

2. Rail and Canal Access, Ground Floor

There were originally three rail lines running east-west and giving access via arched openings to the transit sheds at either side. Each line had two turntables providing access to the train assembly shed to the north. Platforms that served these lines survive in the north-west and north-east corners of the Granary.

Two canal arms formerly ran beneath the ground floor in a roughly north-south direction. No evidence of access trapdoors survives on the platforms but relieving arches are visible just above ground level in the external north wall of the Granary.

3. Hoists, Hatches and Chutes

The layout of the Granary's six floors is illustrated in *Fig. 1*. On floors one to five all the hatch openings have been infilled, apart from the chutes to the exterior on the north and south elevations.

(i) *Roof Hoists*

Three wooden gantries survive on the roof, each with a small wooden pulley room beneath. These have had their mechanisms removed but two pairs of pulley wheels remain above each cubicle and there are a further two pairs positioned on each gantry over rope guides set in the roof.

(ii) *Hatches and Chutes*

On floors one to five there are six single hatches (marked C on the diagram) directly beneath the pulley wheels on the roof gantries.

THE GRANARY
Internal Layout (not to scale)

KEY:

A   Roof gantries and pulley houses
B   Cast iron columns
C   Small hatches
D   Large hatches
E   Sack chutes (removed)
F   Intake doors
G   Openings at locations of
H   Openings for signal pulley wires
J   Hydraulic pipework remnants and locations
K   Enclosed iron pipe
L   Sack chutes to exterior (extant)
M   Electric lifts
N   Loading platforms
O   Railway turntable locations (not visible)
P   Underground canal arms (infilled)
Q   Canal hatch locations
R   Shunting cable runners
S   Stairwell
T   Sidings to west transit shed
U   Sidings to train assembly arcade
V   Sidings to east transit shed
W   Sack hoist pulley housings.

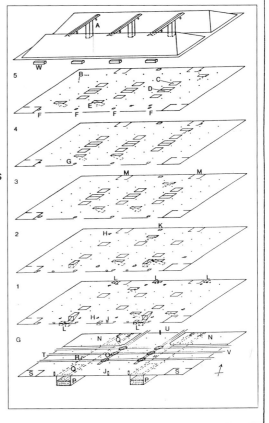

90. The internal layout of the Granary (G1).

On floors three, four and five there are three double hatches (marked D on the diagram) located between the single hatches.

A system of sack chutes formerly connected all floors. Sacks could be transferred from the fifth floor to the ground at the rear of the Granary by progressive east-to-west chutes, ending above the western access line to the train assembly shed. Two sets of chutes near the front of the building allowed a similar transfer of sacks from west to east, ending above the southern ground floor loading platform.

Loading chutes on the first and second floors also gave access to the exterior of the Granary to north and south.

On all floors there are numerous small holes and rectangular openings, presumed to relate to some form of signalling wires and pulleys.

4. Evidence of Hydraulic Machinery
A major feature of the Granary was its early use of hydraulic power for operating hoists, though little evidence of this remains.

(i) *Pipework and Wallfittings*
On the ground floor there are three sections of heavily flanged pipe emerging from the floor at the front of the Granary. Adjacent wall markings and projecting stone corbels delineate probable locations for the hydraulic jiggers which operated the hoists. On the fifth floor there are hoist pulleys above the loading bays on the front elevation.

(ii) *Floor Openings*
On floors one to five there are openings which may relate to the locations of hydraulic jiggers.

5. Ancillary Features

Fireproof doors remain in both stairwells on every floor.

A portable weighing machine with cast-iron frame and wheels, and bearing the letters 'G.N.R.S.' remains in the Granary.

AREAS G2, G3: TRANSIT SHEDS, UNDERGROUND STABLES AND GOODS OFFICES

These two 580-foot long sheds flank the Granary though they are slightly earlier in date. They were built as mirror images in plan and were intended for transhipment of goods between rail, road and canal; the eastern shed being used for trains arriving, the western one for those departing. Both sheds originally featured a central platform with a cart road on one side and a single rail line on the other from which numerous turntables gave access to train assembly sidings situated between the sheds (Area G4). Hatches at the south end of each platform gave access to underlying canal arms connected to the basin in front of the Granary. Much of the space beneath the platforms was occupied by stables for the GNR's cart horses.

The two office buildings in front of the transit sheds were a later addition.

FEATURES

The rails and platforms have been removed from both sheds, the canal arms infilled and the original timber roof trusses replaced in steel. However, the main structure of both sheds survives with only a few additional or enlarged door openings, and their colossal interior space is only subdivided by superficial partition walls.

1. Door Runners and Timbers

Some of the door openings retain original timber supports and cast-iron runners for sliding doors.

2. Clock – Western Transit Shed

A large clock face is set in the northern gable wall. (The clock mechanism and weights may remain in situ but were not accessible.)

3. Stables beneath Transit Sheds

(i) *Fireproof Construction*

Originally, two cast-iron columns supported a single cast-iron beam dividing each bay, but half the width of the roof has been demolished and replaced by rolled steel joists and a concrete ceiling. The columns are slender with no ornamentation, and the beams have an inverted V-section with rectangular recesses in the underside. The beams carry low brick vaults and are linked by wrought-iron tie-rods. This fireproof construction is unusual for the King's Cross site, timber joists and floors in general being preferred.

(ii) *Former Tunnel Access*

A brick arched tunnel linked the stables to the low level yard on the east side of the adjacent coal drops. The tunnel is now sealed off where it meets the stables.

(iii) *Waggon Turntable Bases*

The eastern wall incorporates two semi-circular brick projections which supported turntables at rail level above.

4. Goods Offices

Access to the eastern offices revealed no major features though some minor fittings remain including cast-iron fire fenders and fire bucket brackets marked 'G.N.R.'

AREA G4: TRAIN ASSEMBLY SHED AND OVERHEAD OFFICES

The area between the two transit sheds was originally occupied by twelve railway lines under an overall roof. The lines were inter-connected with each other and lines in the transit sheds and Granary via numerous turntables. The area was used to assemble trains of loaded or empty waggons released from the transit sheds on either side. In 1897–99 a new range of offices was provided above the railway lines along the west side of the shed. More recent rationalisation saw the removal of the railway lines and provision of a new roof and loading platforms.

FEATURES

1. Cast-Iron Columns

There are eight massive cast-iron columns in a colonnade along the west side of the shed. Each has a raised maker's mark 'W. Richards & Son, Makers, Leicester'. Other colonnades in the shed have rolled steel posts, though all have fabricated piers in their two northernmost bays.

The cast-iron columns correspond to the extent of first floor offices above, and are arranged in a distinctive pattern, alternating with fabricated I-section posts, that matches the 1865 plan by Humber in which the positions of the fabricated posts are occupied by short lengths of wall. When the first floor offices were built the present cast-iron columns were provided in place of less substantial columns supporting the original roof. Subsequently the original lengths of brick wall shown on Humber's plan were replaced by the present pairs of fabricated posts. At the north end of the sheds there are three remaining lengths of brick wall, each with a simple stone cornice.

91. The transit shed, showing the cast-iron columns supporting the first floor offices (G4).

2. Cast-Iron Roof Truss Brackets

A row of 26 cast-iron brackets are set into the western wall beneath the first floor offices. These have the same moulded profile as brackets in the *porte cochère* on the west side of King's Cross passenger terminal, and are characteristic of the early roofs at King's Cross.

92. Composite roof trusses of 1851 re-erected over the first floor offices (G4).

93. The upper floor of Midland Shed (H2).

3. First Floor Offices

These remain substantially intact with an extensive range of accommodation retaining many late 19th century fittings. These include double-hung sash windows throughout, red and ochre tile floor, ceramic sinks, some wooden panelling and solidly built panelled doors.

AREA G5: ACCESS ROADS AND FORECOURT

There are many features of value in the area, including two early waggon turntables in front of the Granary which are particularly important as the only examples known to remain on the site.

The original canal basin (now infilled) occupies the space in front of the Granary, and its outline is delineated by the extent of surrounding cobbles.

AREA H: THE MIDLAND GOODS SHED AND ENVIRONS

This area is considered under three sub-headings:

AREA H1: THE 1888 HANDYSIDE ROOF AND 1850 OFFICES

The area between the Midland goods shed (H2) and eastern transit shed was roofed over in 1888 to give additional cover for the potato market as part of a broader scheme to provide facilities competitive with those of the Midland Railway's potato depot at Somers Town.

The goods offices dating from 1850 have been taken over and refurbished as the site headquarters of the London Regeneration Consortium.

FEATURES
1. 1850 Offices

These have been extensively refurbished inside and out, retaining the cantilevered stairs with decorative cast-iron balusters.

2. Cast-Iron Columns and Fabricated Girders

The 1888 roof is carried on 19 D-section cast-iron columns that stand against the walls of the adjacent sheds. Because of the oblique angle at which the roof abuts the Midland shed, the brickwork here has been stepped out to receive the D-section columns. Each column bears an oval maker's mark reading 'A HANDYSIDE & CO. 1888. DERBY AND LONDON'.

The columns support I-section fabricated diamond-lattice girders of three standard types for spans of different lengths. Only the girder at the north-west corner of the Midland shed is of an individual design.

3. Roof Trusses

The roof is divided into transverse bays by the main girders and each bay has a gabled roof. Each truss is constructed of T-section iron bar and wrought-iron rods. Some of the trusses are truncated because of the angle at which the roof meets the Midland shed.

AREA H2: THE MIDLAND GOODS SHED AND HYDRAULIC ACCUMULATOR TOWER

The Midland goods shed was built as a carriage shed for the temporary GNR terminus at Maiden Lane. However, under an agreement of 1858 its use was altered to provide separate accommodation for Midland Railway goods traffic. This arrangement was short lived and by 1862 the Midland Railway had completed its own coal depot at Agar Town to the west of King's Cross, and was promoting its own line to St Pancras, opened in 1868. The building consists of a ground level transit shed with two loading platforms and a first floor storage space. A three storey row of offices occupies the south elevation.

FEATURES
1. Evidence of Phasing

Substantial evidence of different phases of construction and adaptation is present in the brickwork.

There are bricked-up window openings at ground and first floor on east, north and west elevations, remnants of a projecting extra string course between first and ground floors, and many inserted and enlarged door openings.

Internally there is clear indication of an earlier double gabled roof that preceded the present single ridged structure.

2. Early Cast-Iron Girders
Original openings were spanned by cast-iron beams, some of which survive, either spanning openings or concealed within later brickwork.

3. Inserted Fabricated Girders
These are set at a higher level than the cast-iron beams, and they also intersect several of the bricked-in window openings.

4. Internal Structure and Layout
The shed is divided longitudinally by two short stub walls and a colonnade of massive cast-iron columns, three of which are positioned to provide two longer spans. The columns support lateral and transverse fabricated girders and a wooden floor.

The layout of the goods shed comprises two lines of track separated by the colonnade and with platforms either side. Each platform contains inset loading bays opposite the door openings.

The arrangement of columns, sidings and loading platforms corresponds to that shown on Humber's plan of 1865. In Humber the more southerly of the colonnade's longer spans is occupied by a transverse siding linking the shed roads to the potato market to the east via turntables.

At first floor there is a single uninterrupted floor space with only a few small partitioned offices at the southern end. The current floor level is just above the height of an upper set of windows, many of which have been infilled. At the northern end of the building the floor intersects infilled window openings at different heights. The present internal structure and first floor is evidently a later insertion replacing a floor at a lower level.

5. Taking-in Doors
There are three taking-in doors on the east elevation and two on the west. The former open above the eastern potato market roof and clearly went out of use when the roof was constructed. Of the western ones, the southern door was allowed for when the 1888 roof was built and continued in use, whereas the northern one was infilled and obstructed by the new roof structure.

6. Hydraulic Accumulator Tower
This brick tower and its accumulator are of great importance as the only major remnants of the hydraulic power facility on the goods yard site. The original main accumulator and pumping engines were located south-west of the Granary and were demolished some years ago.

The accumulator and tower post-dates the Humber map of 1865 and pre-dates the 1888 roof. However, the exact date of its construction is not known. It was probably provided as a back-up facility to maintain water pressure in an area of high demand at a distance from the main power source.

The accumulator itself consists of an open iron tank of annular cross section which concentrically surrounds a long, vertical cylinder containing a piston. The top of the tank is attached by its inner edge to the piston head, the outer edge being stayed to the inner by iron plates. The tank is ballasted with a mixture of iron weights and gravel. During operation, water in the cylinder was pressurised by the weight of the laden tank acting on the piston. Variations in demand for power caused the tank to rise and fall with the piston, between automatic valve trip-cocks, and it was constrained by two guide rails on the north and south walls.

AREA H3: POTATO MARKET ROOF
This roof was erected in 1888 on the east side of the Midland shed as part of improvements to the potato market. The open area to the east of the roof was also once covered.
FEATURES
1. Cast-Iron Spandrel Beams
A row of modern rolled I-section posts supports an arcade of 18 cast-iron spandrel beams carrying the eastern side of the roof. The beams survive from the GNR's temporary Maiden Lane passenger terminus and although most of the columns have been lost, the original capitals remain in place linking the beam ends. A nineteenth spandrel beam is set into a short length of brickwork at the arcade's northern end.

2. Roof Structure
The area is covered by a curved, gabled roof supported on trusses attached to brackets on the spandrels and to brackets carried on stone corbels along the east wall of the Midland shed.

3. Tunnel Ventilation Shaft
One of a pair of red brick shafts is located to the east of the roof.

AREA I: THE POTATO MARKET
This area runs parallel to York Way on its western side. The site originally housed the temporary Maiden Lane passenger terminus of 1850 which preceded the King's Cross terminal. The Maiden Lane station was converted into a potato market which was successively enlarged and adapted, particularly during the 1880s. The southern part was demolished in 1970 and most of the northern part in 1988.
FEATURES
1. Cast-Iron Columns and Spandrel Beams
A few original columns and cast-iron beams remain in situ from the Maiden Lane terminus. Some retain fragments of roof members and these have the same detailing and form as other early roofs in the goods yard.

94. Surviving cast-iron column and spandrel beams in the potato market (I).

2. Retaining Wall along York Way

A substantial stock brick wall with recesses and cast-iron railings with fleur-de-lis motifs.

3. Ventilation Shafts

A red brick ventilation chimney stands in this area, and there is a further shaft without a stack, capped by an iron grille, in one of the wall recesses.

4. Cast-Iron Columns

Two cast-iron columns stand at the gateway to the potato market opposite Copenhagen Street. These are the sole survivors of the overall roof that once covered the cobbled roadway between the market and York Way.

AREA J: COAL AND FISH OFFICES, SOUTHERN SECTION OF WHARF ROAD

AREA J1: COAL AND FISH OFFICES

The coal and fish offices were constructed in several phases, the first dating from 1852. The various periods of building are easily distinguished as each rises to a different height. Running from east to west these are: two storey, tall three storey, low three storey, tall single storey, low single storey.

Much of the structure has been gutted by fire and is shored internally.

FEATURES
1. Taller Three Storey Bays

Eight large cast-iron beams support the floor joists. They are of inverted T-section with two beams in each room on the first and second floors.

The main stairway is cantilevered, with plain iron balusters and wooden handrail.

Above the top floor there is a massive iron water tank supported by six I-section beams.

2. Low Three Storey Bays

Cast-iron columns and beams carry the timber floor joists and boards.

J2: WHARF ROAD

This area covers the southern part of the perimeter road, from York Way to the water softening plant in area C.

FEATURES
1. Brick Arch of former Canal Bridge

This brick relieving arch is located in the perimeter wall above the disused inlet to the infilled Granary canal basin. The arch is set over a cast-iron beam visible from the canal towpath.

2. Perimeter Wall

This stock brick wall marks the south and west boundaries of the goods yard.

AREA K: REGENT'S CANAL

The canal was opened in 1820 to link the Grand Junction Canal, which carried traffic from the Midlands, to the London Docks at Limehouse. The presence of the canal dictated the need for the Maiden Lane tunnels (latterly Gasworks tunnels), which always hindered expansion of the King's Cross passenger terminal. The canal also defined the southern limit of the goods yard.

Interchange of traffic with the canal was an integral part of the original 1850s' goods facilities at King's Cross. Canal arms served the Granary and transit sheds via the Granary basin, and the coal traffic was served by the coal and stone basin west of the 1859–60 coal drops.

FEATURES
1. York Way Bridge

The original Maiden Lane bridge survives with a modern concrete extension on its west side. Features remaining on the east elevation include brick abutments with stone cornice and quoins and a cast-iron cornice beam with iron railings above. The span consists of nine cast-iron beams, one pair supporting stone flags, the remainder carrying shallow brick arches.

The quoins, cast-iron cornice and eastern face beam are all similar to those of the canal inlet bridge in Area E.

2. Stop Locks

Two stop locks were installed on either side of the Maiden Lane railway tunnels during the Second World War to minimise loss of water into the tunnels in the event of bomb damage to the canal.

3. Concrete Access Bridge

An inter-war concrete bridge provides access to the yard from Goods Way. It has a cobbled road surface and granite kerbs.

4. Sealed Canal Arm to Granary Basin

This feature is identified in the brickwork of the canal bank retaining wall by a massive cast-iron beam, a brick relieving arch and areas of brick infill.

5. Footings of Railway Bridge to Plimsoll Coal Drops

Six stone blocks set into the wall opposite the Camley Street Natural Park mark the position of the over-bridge to the Plimsoll coal drops (Area L).

6. Towpath Bridge over former Coal and Stone Basin Inlet

This is of cast-iron construction with plain segmental beams. The bridge abutments and towpath wall are brick with stone dressings.

7. St Pancras Locks and Lock-keeper's Cottage

The lock-keeper's cottage was built to serve also as a pumping station to return water to the head of the locks.

8. Evidence of Midland Railway Coal Staithes

Truncated ends of iron girders projecting from the west wall of the St Pancras Yacht Basin are remnants of triple-track coal staithes which used to run above the basin.

AREA L: CAMLEY STREET AND NATURAL PARK

The Camley Street Natural Park occupies the site of coal drops built in 1865–67 by Samuel Plimsoll. On the south-west side of Camley Street is a refuse depot on the site of the Midland Railway coal drops. There are virtually no remains of either coal drop.

FEATURES

1. Gates to Camley Street Natural Park

A substantial pair of wrought-iron gates with gothic detail stand at the entrance to the park. These formerly stood in the Midland Railway goods depot at Somers Town. A smaller side gate has matching detailing.

2. Cast-Iron Column

A single column remains from the Midland Railway coal drops. This is located on the boundary wall between the gas holders and refuse depot.

AREA M: GOODS WAY

The south-western section of Goods Way was formerly part of Wharf Road, which used to cross the canal by Somers Bridge to the east of the coal and fish offices. The later, eastern section of Goods Way runs through the site of the Imperial Gas Light and Coke Company's retort houses.

FEATURES

1. Site of GNR Stables

This is now occupied by the factory and offices of Haden Young. The cobbled area to the west of this is on part of an LNER van yard through which the stables were reached.

2. Gas Works Wall, south side of Goods Way

This stock brick wall runs the entire length of the gasworks area's northern boundary. It contains many phases of brickwork including seven round-headed openings now blocked. These are almost certainly part of a 'Material House' shown on the 1939 version of Goad's Insurance Plan. The east end of the wall marks the former extent of Wharf Road before the construction of Goods Way.

3. Gas Works Wall, north side of Goods Way

A second stock brick wall runs along the perimeter of the northern gasworks area.

4. Midland Railway Retaining Wall

This red brick wall with gothic details stands below the preserved water tower outside St Pancras passenger terminus.

AREA N: GASHOLDERS

This area is subdivided into a northern area (N1) containing gasholders only, and a southern area (N2) which contains gasholders and some remains of the former Imperial Gas Light and Coke Company's works.

AREA N1

FEATURES

1. Group of Three Telescopic Gasholders

These three interlocking guide frames date from the 1880s, erected over tanks of 1861–64. The guide frames comprise cast-iron columns of three vertical sections topped by classical capitals, and braced together by three rows of lattice girders. The telescopic gas tanks are of riveted iron plate: the southern one has been removed.

2. Group of Two Telescopic Holders

Two later holders (post 1883) feature tapered lattice guides, braced by fabricated lattice girders and lacking any decoration.

3. Manual Pumps

Manual pumps with cast-iron crank wheels are located around the bases of the gasholders. They are used to top-up the water level in the tank-sealing ponds.

4. Wrought-Iron Handrail Posts

The safety handrails surrounding the tank wells are supported by spiral wrought-iron uprights.

AREA N2

FEATURES

1. Two Telescopic Gasholders

The northern holder is of similar construction to the interlocking group in Area N1. It has cast-iron columns with classical capitals but is one tier lower than those in the northern area. It bears the date 1883 at the base of one column. The southern holder is of lattice construction similar to holder number 2 in Area N1.

2. Manual Pumps

Each holder has a pump of similar construction to those in area N1.

3. Remains of Gasworks

The former gasworks also extended across areas O, P and Q. Much of the space surrounding the gasholders is covered by loose gravel which could possibly conceal features from the earlier gasworks. The main area of remains lies along the south-east edge of the site where a sunken cobbled roadway runs from a gateway on Battle Bridge Road. Just inside the gateway is the filled-in pit of a weighbridge, and the footings of a recently demolished structure to its west. The low retaining walls of the sunken roadway utilise a rich assortment of old bricks, arch fragments and refractory bricks from the retort ovens of the old gasworks.

AREA O: STABLES, BATTLE BRIDGE ROAD

This area is shown as LNER stables and garages on Goad's insurance plan as updated in 1939. It is located east of the gasholders and is reached from Battle Bridge Road.

There is a long row of older buildings on the west side of the area, with more recent buildings to the east.

FEATURES

1. Northern Stable Block

A brick, two-storey building with a corrugated roof. One of the ground floor doors is of a split stable type with wrought-iron strap hinges. The east ground-floor wall has three circular openings, one of which retains a cast-iron window frame. A central doorway leads to a room with a cobbled floor. The first floor has two taking-in doors, one of which has a hand-winch inside.

2. Southern Stable Block

This two-storey, brick structure is identified as 'Motor Sundries' on Goad's plan, but has a split stable type door in the northern opening. The first floor has unusually long windows, two on the east elevation, and three on the west.

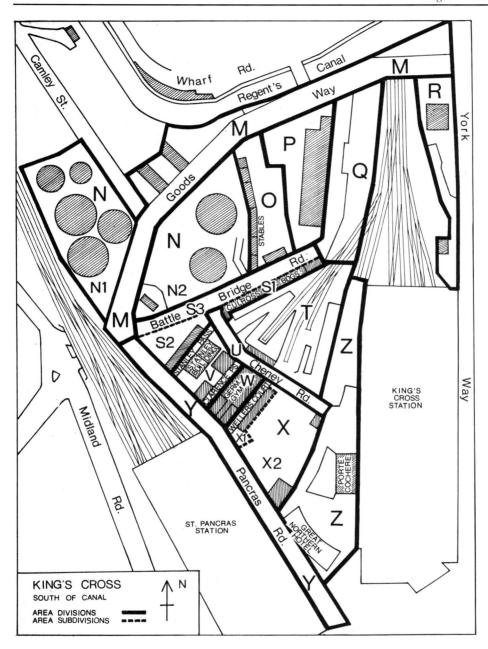

95. *Key plan, south of the canal.*

AREA P: MOTOR MAINTENANCE DEPOT

Located to the east of the stables, this area is reached by a separate gateway from Battle Bridge Road. The area was formerly occupied by the Imperial Gas Light and Coke Company's gasworks, but no surface indications of this remain.

There are now workshops of post-war steel and concrete construction, with a main shed roofed by a series of reinforced concrete vaults.

AREA Q: SITE OF ENGINE DEPOT

This area was formerly occupied by locomotive stabling facilities installed in 1923 after being displaced by the expanding suburban terminus on the west side of King's Cross passenger station. The remains of the 1960s diesel depot include pre-fabricated offices and concrete bases for fuel tanks. There is no evidence of the 70 foot steam locomotive turntable that once stood here.

AREA R: YORK ROAD STATION ENVIRONS

This area lies between York Way and the railway approach to King's Cross terminal. The northern part has modern buildings and a tarmac forecourt. The southern part includes the site of York Road suburban platform, the entrance to the tunnel used by trains to the Metropolitan 'Widened Lines', and an access ramp at the north end of the former cab road.

FEATURES

1. Cobbled Ramps

These ramps give access to the separate York Road station entrance and the east side cab road at King's Cross. The former is flanked by a stone-flagged pavement enclosed by stone-capped brick walls. At the north end of the pavement is a flight of stone steps and a cast-iron lamp standard with a largely intact lamp fitting.

2. St Pancras Parish Boundary Stone

A rectangular stone is set into the brickwork of the York Way wall. It is inscribed 'The Boundary Line of St Pancras Parish Extends 22(?) 3(?) Eastward from the Face of this Stone. 1853.'

3. Cast-Iron Beam

The cast-iron lintel over the York Road tunnel portal still survives in situ.

4. Enginemen's 'Bothy'

This two-storey stock brick structure with slate roof post-dates the demolition of the Battle Bridge Road viaduct which formerly spanned the station throat at this location.

AREA S: BATTLE BRIDGE ROAD, CULROSS BUILD-INGS AND VEHICLE REPAIR DEPOT

This area is considered under three sub-headings:

AREA S1: CULROSS HALL AND CULROSS BUILDINGS

Culross Buildings were built in 1891–92 to provide improved standards of accommodation for workers. Culross Hall was one of three mission halls which the GNR erected along its route as centres for religious guidance and recreation.

FEATURES

1. Culross Hall

The Hall had an integrated heating system which used ducting of galvanised iron to direct warm air around the building. On the first floor warm air was brought in through two types of duct, one supplying a convection current bringing air up from the ground floor rooms, the second type bringing heat directly from the basement. The convection current of warm air was vented through iron ceiling grilles with further ducting to the atmosphere outside.

2. Culross Buildings

No access was obtained to the interior of the flats, but it appears that the majority have been extensively modernised.

(i) *Cast-iron Ash Disposal Chutes*

Each landing was provided with an ash disposal chute covered by an iron flap.

(ii) *Balustrades*

The landings have wrought-iron balustrades of plain rectangular bar.

AREA S2: FORMER MIDLAND RAILWAY ROAD VEHICLE REPAIR SHOP

The original brick building has been abutted by a more recent overall roof covering the former courtyard to the workshop.

FEATURES

1. Perimeter Walls

Red brick walls with recessed panels and some sections of stone capping run along Battle Bridge Road, Cheney Road and the east end of Stanley Passage. The walls retain a pair of wrought-iron gates on the eastern boundary.

2. Workshops

Single storey, red brick building with substantial wall onto Stanley Passage, and a northern elevation of open bays divided by cast-iron columns. The columns support wrought-iron lattice girders which carry a timber roof. The west elevation has a gabled roof, but an additional bay at the eastern end has been given a hipped roof.

AREA S3: BATTLE BRIDGE ROAD

FEATURES

1. Gasworks Wall

This substantial brick wall runs along the north side of the road for much of its length. It is interrupted by inserted openings of various dates.

2. Surfaces

The road surface is cobbled with granite kerbs and some areas of flagstone paving.

AREA T: KING'S CROSS SUBURBAN STATION SIDINGS

As traffic demands increased the passenger facilities had to be expanded to the west side of the main terminus where the only available land was situated. Area T extends from the roofed suburban platforms to the workshops under Culross Buildings.

FEATURES

1. Cheney Road Frontage

A two storey row of offices fronts Cheney Road: its decorative brickwork has details matching those of the earlier German Gymnasium on the opposite side of the road. A similarly decorated boundary wall continues north-west to Culross Buildings.

2. Cast-Iron Column
A slender column with simplified Corinthian capital stands at the end of the sidings immediately north of the 'Hotel Curve' tunnel cutting. It appears to have been re-used and does not match any other columns on the site.

3. Island Platform and Canopy
In 1924 an additional island platform was built on the site of the former engine stabling yard to the west of the present suburban platforms. The truncated southern end of this platform remains and has a canopy with lightweight steel trusses supported on double I-section pillars.

4. 'Hotel Curve' Tunnel and Cutting
To the north-west of the 1924 platform is a single track cutting leading to the portal of the 'Hotel Curve' tunnel. The tunnel allowed suburban trains coming from Moorgate via the 'Widened Lines' to join the departure lines from King's Cross.

5. Horse Wharf
A cobbled platform with gritstone edging stands in the centre of the area. This was recently used as a Motorail terminal, but was formerly used for loading and unloading horsedrawn carriages and other road vehicles.

6. Milk Platforms
This V-plan double platform with sunken central roadway was used for the transfer of milk churns from rail to road. It has a concrete surface with gritstone edging and modern steel and asbestos canopy. A cast-iron lamp standard remains at the east end.

7. Blacksmith's Forge
This small building abuts the eastern end of Culross Buildings. On Goad's insurance plan updated in 1939, it is marked as an electrical accumulator room. It currently contains a cast-iron forge hearth lettered 'Gold Medal. Sydney. No. 478'.

AREA U: CHENEY ROAD
This cobbled street is flanked by the high, decorated brick boundary walls of King's Cross Suburban station, the German Gymnasium and Stanley Buildings.

FEATURES
1. Street Furniture and Surfaces
Notable details include the cobbled road surface, granite kerbs, flagstone pavements and a particularly fine group of six cast-iron marker posts. The latter are of octagonal and square section with raised letters 'S.P.P. 1854' (St Pancras Parish). One unmarked post contrasts with these and is similar to those in Stanley Passage.

AREA V: STANLEY BUILDINGS
The area between Pancras Road and Cheney Road incorporates the three surviving blocks of Stanley Buildings, two empty plots resulting from bomb damage, and a former public house at 32 Pancras Road. It also includes Stanley and Clarence Passages.
   Stanley Buildings were erected in 1864–65 by the Im-

96. Cheney Road (U).

97. Clarence Passage, Stanley Buildings on the right (U).

proved Industrial Dwellings Company to provide a higher standard of workers' housing.

FEATURES
1. Balconies
These are supported on cast-iron columns and beams and have decorated cast-iron balustrades. Each opening on the balconies is flanked by pilasters whose unusually decorated capitals feature an oval emblem and Ionic scrolls.

2. Stucco Work
The ground-floor front elevations have a stucco finish resembling courses of dressed stone work. The main windows have moulded stucco surrounds and pediments carried on consoles. The windows on the first floor have remnants of projecting cills that formerly carried miniature cast-iron balustrades.

3. 32 Pancras Road
This corner building with intricate detailing on the main elevations has been extensively renovated. It combines carved stonework, bands of contrasting coloured brick, stucco pilasters and projecting window cills with miniature cast-iron balustrades. There are also stucco cornices above the ground and second floors.

AREA W: GERMAN GYMNASIUM AND PANCRAS ROAD FRONTAGE

The Gymnasium was built in 1864–65 for the German Gymnastic Society and is particularly important for its rare surviving laminated timber roof ribs which are of similar construction to the original ribs of the King's Cross passenger terminal. The building comprised a gymnasium and subsidiary hall, reached from an imposing doorway in the centre of a symmetrical shop frontage on Pancras Road. The gymnasium has been subdivided by partitions and an inserted first floor.

FEATURES

1. Laminated Timber Roof Ribs

2. Pancras Road Frontage

The impressive arched doorway of the gymnasium is set in the projecting central bay of a shop terrace on Pancras Road. The title 'Turnhalle' is inscribed over the door. Many of the first and second-floor window openings retain relief mouldings or carvings of a bearded face.

3. Gymnasium Hall

A row of cast-iron columns with highly decorated capitals support brick arches carrying a first floor gallery. An inserted first floor is carried on rolled steel beams.

AREA X: WELLER'S COURT AND CAR PARKS

This site between Pancras Road and Cheney Road was occupied in 1865 by a 'Wheel Company's Works', with stables for the GNR to the south-east. The 1883 Ordnance Survey map shows a printing works and cartridge manufacturers occupying the former wheelworks. Today most of the area is used as an open car park, but there are three surviving older buildings.

AREA X1: WELLER'S COURT WAREHOUSE

This three storey building was a printing works in 1883. It extends the full length of Weller's Court behind a Pancras Road frontage that features a round-arched doorway, and stucco imitating dressed stone courses on the ground floor.

FEATURES

1. Phasing Evidence in Brickwork

The Weller's Court elevation shows extensive evidence of newer brickwork around the window openings, much of which appears to have replaced taking-in doors on the first and second floors.

2. Internal Layout

The main access on Weller's Court has a substantial iron lamp bracket projecting over the doorway, which leads onto a stairwell east of a transverse dividing wall. Double sliding fire doors give access from the stairway on all floors.

3. Cast-Iron Columns

Slender iron columns on the ground and first floors support double timber beams, some of which have been replaced by rolled I-section girders.

AREA X2: CAR PARKS

FEATURES

1. B.R.S.A. Club

This single storey building of red brick features terracotta rosary decorations on the pilasters dividing each bay. It also has a detailed cornice, string lines and parapet capping. The north-east elevation reveals remnants of a neighbouring building which may have been part of the GNR stables in Edmund Street.

2. Weighbridge

Located at the rear of the taxi park and at an angle to the Weller's Court warehouse. It is not clear how this related to the former usage of the site.

AREA Y: PANCRAS ROAD

Pancras Road is dominated to the west by the impressive flank wall of St Pancras station. On its east side it has a varied street frontage comprising King's Cross station forecourt, the Great Northern Hotel, and various shop fronts and business premises (areas S, V, W and X).

FEATURES

1. St Pancras Station Undercroft: Vehicle Entrances

At the entrances to the undercroft there are several groups of street furniture, comprising cobbled roadways, granite kerbs, cast-iron bollards, fluted cast-iron parish markers lettered 'St. P.P.M' and granite bollards.

Two cast-iron columnar markers bearing raised letters 'SOMMERS TOWN 1817' each with an associated granite bollard, stand at the northern exit from the undercroft.

AREA Z: WESTERN FORECOURT OF KING'S CROSS STATION

The area is located to the west of the passenger terminal and is dominated by the Great Northern Hotel (see Chapter Four). Other major elements in the area are the overall roof of the suburban platforms and the *porte-cochère* to the front of the original booking offices. The *porte-cochère* was originally free-standing to the west where it faced a wedge-shaped area of gardens in front of the hotel. The garden site is now covered by car parks and a single storey parcels office.

FEATURES

1. Roofed Suburban Platforms

These were built in 1875 and extended westwards in 1895 by the reconstruction of the west wall and construction of a new roof.

A substantial stock brick wall on the west side supports fabricated lattice girders dividing the roof into transverse bays, each of which has a hipped roof.

2. Parcel Transit Area

Between the passenger entrance to the suburban platforms and the main terminal there is a parcels handling area with a roof structure similar to that of the suburban platforms. The northern section has offices above, supported on a complex structure of cast-iron columns, fabricated pillars and cast-iron braces.

3. Porte-cochère

This rectangular roofed area is now used for parcels sorting. The canopy originally served as a cover for road carriages depositing passengers at the main booking hall.

4. Miscellaneous

There are four 'Hayward's Patent Self-Locking Plate' coal covers in the Edmund Street pavement north of the Great Northern Hotel.

Around the outside of the hotel are two types of cast-iron railing. One type has raised letters 'G.N.R.S.' on the stanchions, the other has no lettering but has cast shields bearing embossed lions.

THE GOODS YARD ROOF STRUCTURES

Early Lightweight Roofs
Two early 1850s iron roofs remain, one over the mezzanine offices to the rear of the Granary (Area G4) and the other forming the *porte-cochère* to the west side of the main King's Cross passenger terminal (Area Z). Both roofs have characteristics matched in the original temporary passenger station, where remnants of the roof trusses survived within the structure of the potato market until its recent demolition.

The roof over the mezzanine offices was originally part of the roof to the train assembly shed constructed in 1850, but this was re-positioned in 1897 when the offices were constructed above. There are 42 trusses of wrought-iron with composite rafters consisting of square-sectioned timber centres sandwiched by two wrought-iron plates. Tie-rods across the base of each truss are cambered and have central ornamental bosses at the intersection of a central suspension rod and two diagonal raking struts. Each truss has a total of five suspension rods and four diagonal struts. Cast-iron brackets, that once supported the trusses in their original position over the train assembly shed, remain in the eastern wall of the adjacent transit shed. These have a moulded profile which matches brackets for the roof trusses on the two other 1850 roofs.

The *porte-cochère* has a similar truss construction, but the wooden centres are not continuous and their sandwiching iron plates are of L-section, not flat. Also, the tie-rods are not cambered.

The ends of similar composite rafters and iron tie-rods remain attached to the surviving spandrel beams of the temporary Maiden Lane terminus.

The Development of Composite Roofs at King's Cross
Many of the goods yard buildings built between 1850 and the close of the 19th century bear composite roof structures. As successive buildings were constructed distinctive common characteristics evolved, producing a series of roofs which, collectively, illustrate the modification of a single, original set of design practices. This chain of development is not simply of interest in relation to the goods yard, but is extremely important to a broader understanding of 19th-century roofing techniques.

Buildings that form part of this series and have surviving original roofs include The Granary (1851–52), Eastern Coal Drops (1851), Western Coal Drops (1859–60) and the Western Goods Shed (1897–99). The Western Goods Shed is of further interest for its continuation of comparatively archaic mid–19th century roofing practices. The two transit sheds of 1850 have unfortunately lost their original roofs.

Each successive roof made use of less timber in favour of wrought-iron rods and cast-iron brackets and braces. Initially iron was used only for roof members subjected to tension, but the later roofs used, first cast-iron, then T-section wrought-iron for struts under compression.

The Granary's hipped roof makes use of timber for all of its members except for a single wrought-iron suspension rod running down from the apex to the collar in each truss. However, instead of employing complex timber joints the roof makes extensive use of cast-iron brackets at the intersection of timbers.

The roof timbers in the eastern coal drops have wooden tie-beams, rafters, collars and struts, and retain the single iron rod from the apex; but they also have queen posts of wrought iron. In addition, the principal rafters are formed of two timbers joined at collar height by a cast-iron bracket. Wrought-iron plates are also used at the joints.

By 1859–60 when the western coal drops were constructed, the use of iron had increased significantly, being used for roof members in both tension and compression. Wrought-iron tie-bars are used instead of timber, the queen posts are of wrought-iron plate, and cast-iron diagonal struts work in compression between the principal rafters and tie-bars. The ends of the struts also bracket joints between sections of the tie-bar and the wrought-iron queen posts.

In the western goods shed many of the latter principles remain, but the trusses are of greater complexity. The timber collar and two-part timber rafters are retained, as is the primitive method of tying the two halves together using cast-iron brackets. Wrought-iron tie-rods are also used, but the wrought-iron plate queen posts used in the western coal drops are replaced by six wrought-iron suspension rods, and the cast-iron struts replaced by four T-section wrought-iron struts. The offices over the shed have a simplified version of this structure applied to a shorter span.

Other roofs built at this time elsewhere in the country, and even earlier during the 1870s and 1880s, were making use of T-section wrought-iron throughout in trusses of fabricated lattice construction, capable of spanning greater distances using lighter weight structures. In contrast the roof of the western goods shed is a curiously late modification of the earlier mid–19th century roofs used elsewhere on the site.

ROAD SURFACES AND STREET FURNITURE
Throughout the King's Cross site there are numerous examples of 19th century street furniture and paving surfaces which, in combination, form a valuable contribution to the area's character.

Granite cobbles and kerbs occur in virtually every thoroughfare, and in the goods yard there are also cast-iron kerbs of a variety of types, particularly around the western goods shed. Stone paving slabs are slightly less common, but nevertheless they are of additional value in extending the range of 19th century surfaces.

Granite and cast-iron bollards take on a variety of forms and are found in attractive mixed groupings. Notable cast-iron bollards are those in Area J2 marked with the letters G.N.R.S., and the many types of St Pancras parish boundary markers found to the south of the area. Particularly attractive mixed groupings are found on York Way where small granite and taller cast-iron bollards are paired.

GLOSSARY

ACCUMULATOR: an apparatus for accumulating hydraulic power.

ANNULAR: ring-shaped.

BAULK: a roughly squared beam of timber.

CAISSON: a watertight chamber used in underwater construction.

CANTILEVERED: a structure supported by projecting brackets.

CAPSTAN: a cylinder revolving on a vertical axis, used for moving heavy weights and waggons.

CATENARY: a method of hanging overhead wires for electric trains.

CRANK-WHEEL: a wheel used to communicate motion or to change reciprocal into rotary motion.

DERRICK: a contrivance for hoisting and moving heavy weights.

FISH-BELLIED: a beam with a convex lower edge, like a fish's belly.

GALVANISED IRON: iron coated with metal by means of galvanic electricity.

GANTRY: a frame or platform for supporting a crane or similar structure.

GASHOLDER: a tank in which gas is stored ready for distribution.

HOPPER: a receiver shaped like an inverted pyramid or cone through which coal or other loose substances are passed.

JIGGER: a mechanism in which a hydraulic ram operates to power a crane or lift.

LIGHTER: a flat-bottomed barge, normally used for loading or unloading ships which cannot berth alongside a wharf.

LUG: an appendage by which an object may be lifted or suspended.

RETORT-HOUSE: a building used for the production of gas from coal.

ROLLED STEEL JOIST, or R.S.J.: I-section steel joist produced in a rolling mill, first generally available in the 1880s.

ROUNDHOUSE: a circular shed, with a turntable in the centre on which locomotives could be turned around.

SCARF-JOINTED: a method of jointing two timbers longitudinally into a continuous piece by fitting the ends into one another through mutual overlapping.

STOP-LOCKING: a gate by which the water in one section of a canal is shut off from the next in case of damage to the bank.

TRAVERSER: a platform moving laterally on wheels, by which trucks or carriages can be shifted from one set of rails to another.

WARREN TRUSS: a form of girder in which the upper and lower members are connected by struts inclined alternately in opposite directions.

SELECT BIBLIOGRAPHY

R.M. BANCROFT, 'Renewal of the Roof over Departure Platform at King's Cross Terminus GNR', Society of Engineers *Transactions* (1887), 125–140.

W.H. BARLOW, 'On the Roof of St Pancras Station', *Proceedings of the RIBA* (1870–71), 117–30.

T.C. BARKER and MICHAEL ROBBINS, *A History of London Transport*, I (1963), II (1974).

GORDON BIDDLE, *Great Railway Stations of Britain* (1986).

OLIVER CARTER, *An Illustrated History of British Railway Hotels 1838–1983* (1989).

EDWIN COURSE, *London Railways* (1962).

C.H. DENYER ed., *St Pancras through the Centuries* (1935).

ALAN FAULKNER, *The Grand Junction Canal* (1972).

ROGER FINCH, *Coals from Newcastle* (1973).

FOSTER ASSOCIATES, *Master Plan Proposals for the King's Cross Railway Lands* (1988).

GREATER LONDON COUNCIL, *King's Cross and St Pancras, GLC Action Area Draft Local Plan* (1985).

CHARLES H. GRINLING, *History of the Great Northern Railway*, 3rd edn. (1966).

HENRY-RUSSELL HITCHCOCK, *Early Victorian Architecture in Britain*, 2 vols. (1958).

WILLIAM HUMBER, 'On the Design and Arrangement of Railway Stations, Repairing Shops, Engine Sheds etc.', *Minutes of the Proceedings of the Institution of Civil Engineers* XXV (1865–66), 263–91.

ALAN A. JACKSON, *London's Termini*, 2nd edn. (1985).

JOHN R. KELLETT, *The Impact of Railways on Victorian Cities* (1969).

KING'S CROSS RAILWAY LANDS COMMUNITY DEVELOPMENT GROUP, *The King's Cross Development – People or Profit?* (1989).

CHARLES E. LEE, *St Pancras Church and Parish* (1955).

ELLEN LEOPOLD, 'The Impact of Proposals to Develop the King's Cross Railway Lands', *Local Economy* (May 1989), 17–28.

LONDON COUNTY COUNCIL, *Survey of London* XXIV: King's Cross Neighbourhood (Parish of St Pancras Part IV) (1952).

LONDON REGENERATION CONSORTIUM, *King's Cross Extra*, various issues, November 1988 onwards.

DAVID MASTERS, *The Plimsoll Mark* (1955).

GEORGE MEASOM, *Official Illustrated guide to the Great Northern Railway* (1857).

J.MEDCALF, 'King's Cross Goods Station', *Railway Magazine* IV (April 1900), 313–320.

CARROLL L.V. MEEKS, *The Railroad Station. An Architectural History* (1956).

DONALD J. OLSEN, *The Growth of Victorian London* (1976).

GEORGE PAISH, *The British Railway Position* (1952).

GEORGE H. PETERS, *The Plimsoll Line* (1975).

SIMON PEPPER, 'Ossulston Street: Early LCC Experiments in High Rise Housing 1925–29', *London Journal* VII (Summer 1981), 45–64.

JEFFREY RICHARDS AND JOHN M. MACKENZIE, *The Railway Station. A Social History* (1986).

JACK SIMMONS, *St Pancras Station* (1968).

JACK SIMMONS, *The Railway in England and Wales 1830–1914. The System and its Working* (1978).

JACK SIMMONS, 'Suburban Traffic at King's Cross', *Journal of Transport History* 3rd ser. VI (1985), 71–78.

JACK SIMMONS, *The Railway in Town and Country 1830–1914* (1986).

RAYMOND SMITH, *Sea-Coal for London* (1961).

JOHN SUMMERSON, *Victorian Architecture. Four Studies in Evaluation* (1970).

P.N. TOWNEND, *Top Shed. A Pictorial History of King's Cross Locomotive Depot* (1975).

THE VICTORIAN SOCIETY, *Opportunity or Calamity? The King's Cross Railway Lands Development* (1988).

R. WEATHERBURN, 'Railways and Hydraulic Power', *Railway Magazine* XIV (April 1904), 265–78.

JOHN WROTTESLEY, *The Great Northern Railway* I, *Origins and Development* (1979); II, *Expansion and Competition* (1979); III, *Twentieth Century to Grouping* (1981).